NEBRASKA Cookbook

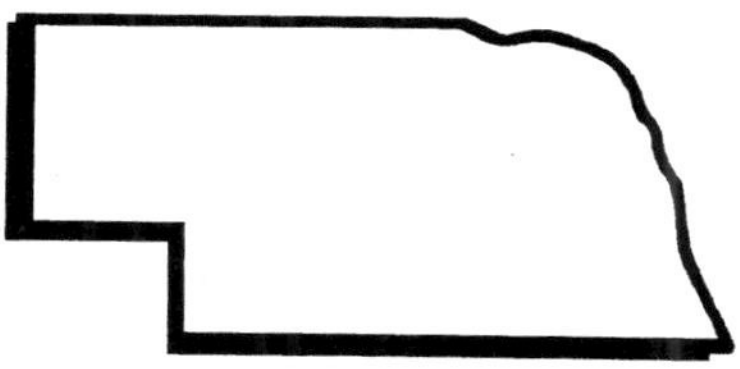

Golden West Cookbooks

Acknowledgments
Special thanks to Mr. Wayne Price of the Nebraska Rural Electric Association whose assistance made it possible for many of our contributors to be included in this book.

Printed in the United States of America

ISBN: 978-1-885590-78-7

2019 Printing

Golden West Cookbooks
5738 North Central Avenue
Phoenix, AZ 85012-1316
800-521-9221

For free sample recipes and complete Table of Contents for every Golden West cookbook, visit: goldenwestcookbooks.com

Contents

Introduction

Welcome to the Cornhusker State! Nebraska is a land of incredible beauty, rich history and friendly people. From pioneer times when intrepid travelers crossed through Nebraska on the Oregon, California and Mormon Trails, to the present day with modern cities, family and corporate farms and charming small towns, this state has offered a diverse array of culinary options. With its Old World influences and Old West roots, Nebraska favorites range from mouth-watering steaks and chuck wagon favorites to modern Continental cuisine.

This Nebraska Cook Book features many ethnic specialties, such as *Polska Kielbasa Soup, Goulash & Dumplings, Kraut Runza* (Beef and Cabbage-Filled Rolls), *Bohemian Christmas Bread* and *Kolaches.* Western favorites include *Cowboy Casserole, Grilled Beef Steak, Mom's Barbecue, Grandpa's Beans* and *Son-of-a-Gun Beef Stew.* You'll also find tasty recipes for *Refrigerator Pickles, Picadilly, Tomato Preserves, Crab Apple Jelly* and *Rhubarb-Pineapple Jam.* Plus many more mouthwatering delights!

Whether you're visiting Nebraska for the first time or have lived here all your life, you're sure to find recipes that will bring back fond memories and offer new delights that are destined to become favorites for your family!

Nebraska Facts

Size—16th largest state with an area of 77,348 square miles
Population—1,920,076 (2017) Ranked #38 in U.S.
State Capital—Lincoln
Statehood—March 1, 1867; the 37th state admitted to the Union
State Nickname—Cornhusker State
State Motto—*Equality Before the Law*
State Flower—Goldenrod
State Song—*Beautiful Nebraska*, written by Jim Fras and Guy G. Miller; music by Jim Fras
State Elevations—*Highest:* southwestern Kimball County—5,426 ft.
Lowest: Richardson County—840 ft.

State Bird
Western Meadowlark

State Insect
Honeybee

State Tree
Cottonwood

Famous Nebraskans

Grace Abbott, *social worker;* Fred Astaire, *dancer/actor;* Max Baer, *boxer;* Marlon Brando, *actor;* William Jennings Bryant, *politician*; Warren Buffett, *investor;* Johnny Carson, *TV entertainer;* Willa Cather, *author;* Dick Cavett, *TV entertainer;* Dick Cheney, *Vice President*; James Coburn, *actor;* Sandy Dennis, *actor;* Mignon Eberhart, *author;* Harold Edgerton, *inventor;* Ruth Etting, *singer/actress;* Henry Fonda, *actor;* Gerald R. Ford, *38th U.S. president;* Bob Gibson, *baseball player;* Hoot Gibson, *actor;* Leland Hayward, *producer;* L. Ron Hubbard, *author*; David Janssen, *actor;* Frank W. Leahy, *football coach;* Harold Lloyd, *actor;* Malcolm X, *civil rights advocate;* Dorothy McGuire, *actress;* Nick Nolte, *actor;* Tom Osborne, *football coach*; Roscoe Pound, *educator/legal scholar;* Red Cloud, *Indian rights advocate and leader;* Mari Sandoz, *author;* Nicholas Sparks, *author*; Standing Bear, *Indian rights advocate and leader;* Hilary Swank, *actor*; Robert Taylor, *actor;* Paul Williams, *singer/composer/actor;* Darryl F. Zanuck, *film producer.*

Nebraska Division of Travel and Tourism: (402) 471-3796
Website: www.visitnebraska.com

Appetizers & Beverages

Nebraska Chicken Wings

"This recipe was passed down to me from my grandmother. I serve them at Sunday meals and they disappear like hot cakes!"

Mary Jo Karnopp—McCool Junction

1 1/2 lbs. **Chicken Wings**, disjointed with tips discarded
Garlic Salt to taste

Sauce:

1/2 cup **Nebraska Wild Plum Jelly**
3 tbsp. **Soy Sauce**
2-3 drops **Hot Pepper Sauce**
1 tbsp. **Mustard**
1 tbsp. **Horseradish** (optional)

Place wings on a baking sheet covered with parchment paper; sprinkle with garlic salt. In a small bowl, combine remaining ingredients and brush generously over wings. Bake at 350 degrees for 35 minutes, basting frequently with sauce.

Mooter's Pimento Cheese Spread

"This recipe is from my father and is a Thanksgiving and Christmas holiday tradition in the Mooter family. It is very different, and we think it's much better than the pimento spread that is purchased at the store."

David Mooter—Kennard

1 package (8 oz.) **Extra Sharp Cheddar Cheese**, grated
1 package (8 oz.) **Cream Cheese**, softened
1 jar (4 oz.) **Pimentos**
3-4 tbsp. **Mayonnaise**
1/4 cup chopped **Stuffed Green Olives**
2-3 **Green Onions**, sliced

In a food processor, blend together cheddar cheese, cream cheese, pimentos and enough mayonnaise to reach the consistency of a spread. Stir in olives and green onions. Add additional mayonnaise as needed for consistency. Refrigerate until ready to serve. Serve with crackers or celery sticks.

Willa Cather

In the late 19th and early 20th centuries, author Willa Cather immortalized life on the Great Plains. Celebrating this heritage the Thematic District in Red Cloud and Webster County encompasses more than 190 sites, making it possibly the largest historic district dedicated to an author in the United States.

Laura's Guacamole

"This is a recipe I developed for a Spanish class project when I was at Chadron High School."

Laura A. Hawthorne—Chadron

1 **Avocado**, peeled and finely chopped
1 **Onion**, finely chopped
1 **Tomato**, finely chopped
1/2 tsp. **Salt**
1/4 tsp. **Pepper**
1/4 tsp. **Garlic Powder**
1/2 tsp. **Chili Powder**
1/4 cup **Salsa**

In a medium bowl, combine avocado, onion and tomato. Gently stir in spices until blended. Stir in salsa. Chill for at least 1 hour to allow flavors to blend. Serve with tortilla chips.

Deep-Fried Morel Mushrooms

Claudeen Penry—Elkhorn Valley Drilling, Inc., Atkinson

1/2 lb. **Morel Mushrooms**, soaked and rinsed thoroughly
3-4 **Eggs**
1 package **Club Crackers**, finely crushed

Place a colander inside a large bowl and place mushrooms in the colander. In a small bowl beat eggs. Pour 1/2 the eggs over mushrooms and mix well. Add the remaining eggs and mix until mushrooms are well-coated. Pour cracker crumbs into a large resealable plastic bag; place mushrooms in bag. While sealing the bag, blow air into it, so that the bag does not cling to the mushrooms. Gently shake to coat mushrooms with crumbs. Deep-fry in hot oil for 1-2 minutes or until batter is golden brown; drain on paper towels. Serve warm.

President Gerald R. Ford

In 1974, "Jerry" Ford, who was born in Omaha, became the 38th President of the United States upon the resignation of President Richard M. Nixon.

Best Ever Chicken Wings

L. Z. Mann—Omaha

40 **Chicken** Wings

Sauce:

1 cup **Sugar**
1 cup **Brown Sugar**
1 bottle (14 oz.) **Ketchup**
1 can (8 oz.) **Tomato Sauce**
1 cup **Cider Vinegar**
4 tbsp. **Worcestershire**
1 tsp. **Dry Mustard**
2-3 drops **Hot Pepper Sauce**

Cut chicken wings apart; discard tips. Prepare a 15 × 11 baking pan with cooking spray and place chicken in pan. In a bowl, combine all sauce ingredients and pour over chicken. Cover and bake at 400 degrees for 1 1/2 hours, remove cover and continue to bake for 1 more hour.

Delicious Dried Beef Dip

"This recipe is representative of Nebraska because Nebraska is beef country. This dip tastes even better served the day after making it, when the flavors have blended."

Julie Lueshen—Wisner

1 package (8 oz.) **Cream Cheese**, softened
1 carton (8 oz.) **Sour Cream**
1 jar (5 oz.) **Dried Beef**, finely chopped
1 small bunch **Green Onions**, sliced
1 **Green Bell Pepper**, finely chopped
1/2-1 tsp. **Garlic Powder**
1/2-1 tsp. **McCormick® Broiled Steak Seasoning Salt**

In a medium bowl, combine cream cheese and sour cream and blend well. Stir in dried beef, green onions and bell pepper. Add garlic powder and seasoning salt. Serve with pretzels, crackers or cocktail rye bread.

Cheese Frenchees

"I had fun making these little sandwiches with my grandma when I was young. They are a great variation on grilled cheese sandwiches. We would make batch after batch and invite the whole family over to share our simple but impressive appetizer."

Kirsten Vala—Vala's Pumpkin Patch, Gretna

6 slices **Sandwich Bread**
Mayonnaise
6 slices **Velveeta**®
1 **Egg**
1/2 cup **Milk**
3/4 cup **Flour**
1 tsp. **Salt**
1 cup crushed **Corn Flakes**

Make three sandwiches using bread, mayonnaise and Velveeta slices. Cut each sandwich into quarters. In a shallow dish, beat together egg, milk, flour and salt. Dip sandwiches in batter to coat all sides. Place cornflake crumbs on a plate and press all sides of sandwiches into crumbs. In a deep-fat fryer, cook at 375 degrees for 2-3 minutes or until golden brown.

Vino Pampeliskove

(Dandelion Wine)

"As a small girl, I helped pick the dandelions whenever Grandpa wanted to make this wine."

Carolyn Wilkens—Gibbon

5 gallons **Water**
6 **Lemons**, cut into pieces
12 **Oranges**, cut into pieces
2 lbs. **Raisins**
20 lbs. **Sugar**
5 quarts **Dandelion Blossoms**
2 cakes **Yeast**

In a large kettle, bring water to a boil; let cool slightly. In a separate stainless steel pot, combine remaining ingredients, except yeast. Pour hot water over mixture; stir in yeast. Cover with a clean cloth and let stand for 10 days; strain. Ferment for 4 weeks. Pour wine into jugs or bottles, cover and store in a cool place.

Party Meatballs

"This is always a favorite family recipe."

Michelle Teegerstrom—Stromsburg

Meatballs:

1 1/2 lbs. **Ground Beef**
3/4 cup **Oatmeal**
2 tbsp. chopped **Onion**
1 **Egg**, beaten lightly
1/2 cup **Milk**
1 1/2 tsp. **Salt**
1/4 tsp. **Pepper**

Sauce:

1/4 cup diced **Onion**
1/4 tsp. **Garlic Salt**
1 tbsp. **Margarine**, melted
3 tbsp. **Vinegar**
4 tsp. **Worcestershire Sauce**
1 tsp. **Salt**
1 tsp. **Paprika**
1/2 tsp. **Pepper**
1 3/4 cups **Ketchup**
1/2 cup **Water**

In a large bowl, combine meatball ingredients and mix well; roll into 1-inch balls and place in a baking pan. Brown in oven at 350 degrees for 10-15 minutes. In a medium bowl, combine sauce ingredients. Place meatballs in a crockpot and cover with sauce. Stir to coat well. Simmer on low for 30 minutes or until done.

Ginger Tea

"This is a medicinal recipe that my daughter-in-law gave me. I keep a jar of it made up at all times. Warm the tea and sip slowly to help with sinus congestion, sore throat or upset stomach."

Claudeen Penry—Elkhorn Valley Drilling, Inc., Atkinson

1 (2-inch) piece **Gingerroot**, thinly sliced
1/2 tsp. whole **Allspice**
1 quart **Water**
1/4 cup packed **Brown Sugar**

In a 2-quart saucepan, combine gingerroot, allspice and water. Simmer over low heat for 30 minutes; strain. Stir in brown sugar. Pour into a glass jar and keep refrigerated.

Nebraska's State Soft Drink

In the 1920s, Edwin Perkins of Hastings developed a concentrated drink mix called "Fruit Smack." In 1927 he dehydrated his product, put it in packets and renamed it "Kool-Aid®."

Sandhills Special Punch

"This punch has been served at a wide variety of family gatherings for many years."

Shawna M. Naranjo—North Platte

2 packages (6 oz. ea.) **Strawberry Jell-O®**
4 cups **Sugar**
4 cups **Boiling Water**
9 cups **Cold Water**
2 tbsp. **Lemon Juice**
2 cans (46 oz. ea.) **Pineapple Juice**
1 bottle (2 liters) **7-Up®**

In a large saucepan, combine Jell-O and sugar with boiling water and stir until dissolved. In a large container, combine cold water, lemon juice and pineapple juice; stir in Jell-O mixture and mix well. Place container in freezer and freeze until solid. When ready to serve, place frozen mixture in a large punch bowl. Add 7-Up and let mixture thaw until slushy.

Breakfasts & Brunches

Apfel Küchen

(Apple Coffee Cake)

"My great-grandmother brought this recipe from Germany."

Linda Giese—West Point

2 cups **Flour**
4 tsp. **Baking Powder**
Pinch of **Salt**
4 tbsp. **Shortening**, melted
1 cup **Milk**
4-6 cups sliced **Apples**
1 1/2 tsp. **Cinnamon**

Topping:

1 cup **Flour**
1 cup **Sugar**
1/2 cup **Margarine** or **Butter**

In a bowl, combine flour, baking powder, salt, shortening and milk and mix well. Pour batter into a greased 13 × 9 baking pan. Cover with apples; sprinkle with cinnamon. In a small bowl, combine flour and sugar; cut in margarine until crumbly. Spread mixture evenly over the apples. Bake at 350 degrees for 25-30 minutes or until apples are soft.

Caramel Scones

"When I was in high school, I boarded with a lady who made these for breakfast. I made them for all seven of my children and they were always a favorite!"

Juanna Beth Lewis—Ainsworth

10 refrigerator **Biscuits**
3/4 cup packed **Brown Sugar**
1/4 cup **Margarine**
3 tbsp. **Light Cream**

Preheat oven to 450 degrees. Place biscuits in a round 9-inch baking pan and place in oven. Meanwhile, in a small saucepan, heat brown sugar, cream and margarine, stirring well. Bring just to a boil. Immediately pour brown sugar mixture over biscuits. Continue baking for 8-10 minutes or until golden brown. Serve warm.

Apple-Sausage Coffee Cake

Nebraska Pork Producer's Council—Lincoln

4 **Sausage Patties**
2 **Tart Apples**, peeled and
sliced 1/4-inch thick
2 tbsp. **Brown Sugar**
1 tsp. **Cinnamon**
1 tbsp. **Butter**
1 1/2 cups **Pancake Batter**

In a large skillet, sauté sausage until browned. Pour off any fat from skillet, add apple slices, sprinkle with brown sugar and cinnamon. Sauté 1-2 minutes until apples just lose their crispness. Set aside. Place butter in a well-seasoned 9-inch iron skillet and heat in a 450 degree oven until bubbly and hot. Arrange sausage patties in pan and cover with apples, distributing evenly. Pour the pancake batter over the apples and bake at 450 degrees until browned, about 8-15 minutes. Cut into pie-shaped wedges and serve immediately.

Christmas Morning Casserole

"We serve this casserole every Christmas."

Deb Wiegert—Beemer

1 package (32 oz.) frozen **Hash Brown Patties**, thawed
4 **Eggs**
1 can (10.75 oz.) **Cream of Mushroom Soup**
2/3 cup **Milk**
2 cans (4 oz. ea.) **Mushrooms**
2 tbsp. **Butter**, melted
2 cups cooked, cubed **Ham**
2 cups shredded **Cheddar Cheese**

In a 13 x 9 baking pan, layer hash brown patties. In a bowl, beat together eggs, soup and milk. Stir in mushrooms, butter and ham. Pour mixture over hash browns and sprinkle top with cheddar cheese. Bake at 375 degrees for 45 minutes.

Our Favorite Coffee Cake

Gail Talbott—Hoskins

Cake:

1 1/2 cups **Flour**
3/4 cup **Sugar**
2 1/2 tsp. **Baking Powder**
3/4 tsp. **Salt**
1/4 cup **Margarine**, softened
3/4 cup **Milk**
1 **Egg**

Streusel:

1/2 cup packed **Brown Sugar**
2 tsp. **Cinnamon**
2 tbsp. **Margarine**, melted
1/2 cup finely chopped **Nuts** (optional)

In a large mixing bowl, blend together all cake ingredients. In a small bowl, combine topping ingredients and mix well. Grease a round 9-inch or an 8-inch square baking pan. Spread half of the cake batter in the pan; sprinkle with half of the streusel; repeat layer with remaining batter and streusel. Bake at 350 degrees for 25-30 minutes or until a toothpick inserted in the center comes out clean.

Honey-Pineapple Syrup

"We use this at some of our church pancake suppers."

Gladys L. Wyatt—Harrisburg

2 cups **Honey**
1 cup **Sugar**
1 cup **Pineapple Juice**
2 tbsp. **Lemon Juice**
1 stick **Cinnamon**

In a saucepan, combine all ingredients and mix well. Bring to a boil. Reduce heat and simmer over low heat for 15 minutes. Remove from heat and discard cinnamon stick; let cool. Pour into bottles or jars, seal and refrigerate.

Scrambled Egg Casserole

Shirley Schmidt—Juniata

1/2 cup **Butter**
2 tbsp. **All-Purpose Flour**
1/2 tsp. **Salt**
1/8 tsp. **Pepper**
2 cups **Milk**
1 cup shredded **American Cheese**
1 cup cubed, cooked **Ham**
1/4 cup sliced **Green Onions**
6 **Eggs**, beaten
1 can (4 oz.) **Mushroom Stems and Pieces**, drained
1 1/2 cups **Soft Bread Crumbs**

In a saucepan, melt 2 tablespoons butter and add flour, salt and pepper; cook and stir until mixture begins to bubble. Gradually stir in milk; cook until thickened, stirring constantly. Remove from heat; add cheese, mix well and set aside. In a large skillet, sauté ham and onions in 3 tablespoons butter until onions are translucent; add eggs. Cook over medium heat, stirring occasionally, until eggs begin to set. Add cheese mixture and mushrooms; mix well. Pour into a greased 11 × 7 baking dish. Melt remaining butter; toss with bread crumbs and sprinkle over top of casserole. Cover and refrigerate for several hours or overnight. Warm to room temperature 30 minutes before baking. Bake, uncovered, at 350 degrees for 25-30 minutes or until top is golden brown.

Schramm Park State Recreation Area

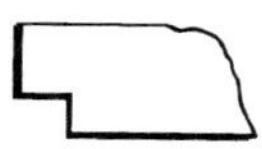

Schramm Park, just south of Gretna, is a 331-acre park on the banks of the Platte River. Here you can find Ak-Sar-Ben Aquarium – 12 tanks displaying native fish in their natural habitats, a large terrarium, and outdoor gardens featuring native plants and flowers that attract butterflies and hummingbirds.

Sunday Egg Bake

"This is my version of an old recipe from family reunions. My family really enjoys this!"

Maxine McCarthy—McCarthy Farms, Naper

12 slices **Bread**
4 1/2 cups diced **Ham**
1 can (4 oz.) **Mushrooms**, drained
1/2 cup chopped **Green Bell Pepper**
1 1/2 cups shredded **Cheddar Cheese**
1/2 cup chopped **Onion**
12 **Eggs**
3 cups **Milk**
1/2 tsp. **Salt**
1/2 tsp. **Pepper**
1/2 cup **Butter**, melted

Place 6 slices of bread on the bottom of a greased 13 × 9 baking pan. Cover with ham, mushrooms, bell pepper, cheddar cheese and onion. Cube the remaining bread and sprinkle on top. In a bowl, beat together eggs, milk, salt and pepper. Pour mixture over bread; drizzle with butter. Cover and refrigerate overnight. Bake at 350 degrees for 1 hour.

Swedish Pancakes

"During my childhood, Swedish pancakes were a treat to look forward to whenever I spent the night at Grandma's house. She would wake up early and prepare these pancakes just like her grandmother used to. They are served with lingonberry sauce—a traditional Swedish condiment."

Kyla Vala—Vala's Pumpkin Patch, Gretna

5 **Eggs**
2 cups **Milk**
1 cup **Flour**
1/2 tsp. **Salt**
3 tbsp. **Butter**, melted
Lingonberry Sauce

In a large bowl, beat eggs until light. Add milk, flour, salt and melted butter and beat until smooth. Heat a tablespoon of butter in a skillet. Pour in 1/4 cup of the batter and cook pancakes until golden brown; turn and brown the other side. Serve topped with lingonberry sauce.

My Favorite Breakfast Casserole

"This is light and fluffy and so easy to make! Serve with toast and a dish of fruit for a perfect meal."

Norma Jean Skalka—Deweese

12 slices **Bread**
2 cups cooked, cubed **Ham***
6 slices **Cheese**
7 **Eggs**
1/2 tsp. **Salt**
1/2 tsp. **Dry Mustard**
4 cups **Milk**
1/4 cup **Margarine**, melted
4 cups crushed **Corn Flakes**

Grease a 13 × 9 baking pan. Place 6 slices of bread on the bottom of the pan and layer ham over top. Arrange cheese slices on top of the ham. Cover all with the remaining bread. In a bowl, beat eggs until light. Add salt and mustard and beat well. Add milk and beat again. Pour mixture over bread. Place cornflakes in a separate bowl, drizzle with margarine and mix lightly. Spread mixture over top of casserole. Cover and refrigerate overnight. Bake at 350 degrees for 1 hour or until set.

* Note: Cooked crumbled sausage may be substituted for ham.

Top All-American Producer!

Since 1952, the University of Nebraska ranks number one nationally in all sports combined for graduating Academic All-Americans.

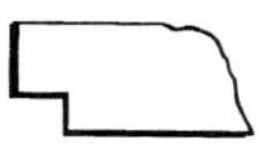

How to Boil an Egg

(Don't Boil It!)

*"My grandmother raised chickens.
She taught me how to boil eggs. If you follow this recipe,
you will have perfect boiled eggs every time!"*

Mitty Quigley—Farm & Ranch, Indianola

Place eggs in a single layer in a pot and cover over by 1 inch with cold water. Bring water to a boil over high heat; turn off heat and cover the pan. Let eggs sit with the lid on for 17 minutes. Drain and run cold water over eggs until they are cool to the touch. Immediately roll each egg until surface is crackled and peel. (Taking the peel off immediately will eliminate the green ring around the yolk.) You can refrigerate peeled eggs in cold water for up to 3 days.

Sour Cream Pancakes & Gravy

"My mother-in-law made these often and I have carried on the family tradition."

Joanne Nitzsche—Bancroft

2 **Eggs**, beaten
1 cup **Milk**
1 1/2 cups **Flour**
1/2 cup **Sour Cream**
1/2 tsp. **Salt**
1 tsp. (rounded) **Baking Powder**
1 tbsp. **Sugar**

In a large bowl, combine all ingredients and beat until smooth; add more sour cream or milk if batter is too thick. Reserve 4 tablespoons batter for gravy. Spoon 3 tablespoons batter onto a hot, ungreased griddle. Using the back of a spoon, spread the batter very thin. Cook for 2-3 minutes until golden brown; turn and cook until golden brown on other side.

Pancake Gravy

1 1/2 cups **Milk**
4 tbsp. reserved **Pancake Batter**
2 tbsp. **Sugar**
Pinch of **Salt**
Cinnamon

In a skillet, heat milk and stir in reserved pancake batter. Add sugar and salt and cook until the mixture thickens; sprinkle with cinnamon to taste. Serve over hot pancakes.

Did You Know?

Nebraska is the only state in the nation with a unicameral (one house) legislature.

Breakfast Cookies

"This recipe is from my grandmother, Dora Creech."

Helen Fleischman—Tekamah

1 cup packed **Brown Sugar**
1 cup **Sugar**
2 **Eggs**
1 cup **Shortening**
2 cups **Flour**
2 tsp. **Baking Powder**
1 tsp. **Baking Soda**
Pinch of **Salt**
2 cups **Corn Flakes**
1 cup **Coconut Flakes**
2 cups **Oatmeal**
1/4 cup **Hot Water**

In a large bowl, cream together both sugars with eggs and shortening. In a separate bowl, mix together flour, baking powder, baking soda and salt; stir in corn flakes, coconut and oatmeal. Blend mixtures together and stir in hot water. Drop batter by rounded teaspoonfuls onto a greased cookie sheet. Bake at 350 degrees for 18 minutes.

Lincoln—the Star City

With a population of only 30, Lancaster (renamed Lincoln in honor of Abraham Lincoln), became the capital of Nebraska in 1867. Between the years 1922-1932, a new capitol building was built around an existing building (which was later torn down). "The Sower," a 19-foot bronze statue with a 14-foot base, stands on top of the 400-foot central tower.

Soups & Salads

Corn & Cabbage Chowder

"I was searching for a chowder recipe that used a combination of vegetables. By combining several recipes into one, I created this hearty dish!"

Helen Syfie—Omaha

2 tbsp. **Margarine**
1 small **Onion**, chopped
2 **Potatoes**, diced
4 cups **Chicken Broth**
1 package (10 oz.) frozen **Corn**
2 cups coarsely shredded **Cabbage**
2 cups **Milk**
Salt and **Pepper** to taste

In a soup pot, melt margarine and sauté onion until golden brown. Stir in potatoes and chicken broth and bring to a boil. Reduce heat, cover and simmer over low heat for 10-15 minutes. Remove 3 cups of potatoes and 1 cup of broth from the soup pot and purée in a blender; stir into soup. Add the corn and cabbage and bring to a boil. Reduce heat and simmer over low heat for 5 minutes. Stir in milk and cook for an additional 5 minutes or until cabbage is tender and mixture is hot; do not overcook! Season with salt and pepper.

Polska Kielbasa Soup

(Polish Sausage Soup)

Jami Talbott—Hoskins

3 large **Potatoes**
4 stalks **Celery**
3 large **Carrots**
2 medium **Onions**
1/2 tsp. **Salt**
1/2 tsp. **Pepper**
2 1/2-3 cups **Water**
1 ring (1 lb.) **Polska Kielbasa Sausage**
1 can (11.5 oz.) **Bean and Bacon Soup**, undiluted

Slice vegetables into bite-size pieces and place in a large soup pot; season with salt and pepper. Add water and cook over medium heat for 30 minutes or until vegetables are tender. Peel sausage and cut into bite-size pieces. Stir in sausage and bean and bacon soup. Heat thoroughly.

Chicken & Noodles Soup

"My mother taught me how to make this dish. Grandma Hunt, who raised chickens and cows to provide meat, eggs, cream and milk for her family, passed her noodle recipe on to my mother."

Liana Rich—Culbertson

1 (4-5 lb.) **Stewing Chicken**
Water
1 stalk **Celery**, with leaves, diced
1 **Carrot**, diced
1/2 cup diced **Onion**
1/4 tsp. **Celery Seed**
1 tsp. **Salt**
1/4 tsp. **Garlic Powder**
1/2 tsp. **Onion Powder**
2 tbsp. **Flour**

Place chicken in a 5-quart Dutch oven or stew pot and add water to within 2 inches of top. Add celery, carrot, onion, celery seed, salt and 1/2 of the garlic powder and bring to a boil. Reduce heat, cover and simmer over low heat for 2-3 hours or until chicken is tender, adding water as needed to keep chicken covered. Remove chicken from pan, cool and debone. Reserve broth and refrigerate. When broth is cool, skim fat from surface. Add additional water or a can of chicken broth (for richer flavor) and bring to a boil. Add Grandma Hunt's Noodles, stirring to prevent noodles from sticking together. Simmer over medium heat for 25-30 minutes or until noodles are done. Stir in onion powder and remaining garlic powder. In a bowl, combine a small amount of broth with flour and stir into broth. Add chicken and heat thoroughly.

Grandma Hunt's Noodles

3 **Eggs**
1 tbsp. **Cream**
1 tsp. **Salt**
3 cups **Flour**

In a bowl, beat together eggs, cream and salt. Stir in flour until mixture forms a soft dough. On a lightly floured surface, roll dough into a thin rectangular shape. Let dry for 2 hours; cut into noodles. Use immediately or freeze for later use.

Serving suggestion: **Chicken & Noodles** is also great served over mashed potatoes!

Czarnina

(Polish Duck Soup)

"I remember as a young girl going to my JaJa's (Grandpa's) house. My aunt always made Czarnina for Sunday dinner during the winter months. It was delicious."

Marcene Kaslon—Ashton

1 large **Duck**
3 stalks **Celery**, chopped
1 **Onion**, diced
Salt to taste
3 tbsp. **Flour**
1/4 cup **Sugar**
1/4 cup **Water**
2 cups **Duck Blood**
2 cups **Prunes**
2 cups **Raisins**
2 **Apples**, chopped

In a soup pot, cover duck with water. Add celery, onion and salt and bring to a boil. Reduce heat and cook over low heat for 1 1/2 hours or until duck is tender. Remove duck from broth, debone and cut meat into bite-size pieces. Skim fat from top of broth and bring broth back to a boil. In a bowl, whisk together flour, sugar, salt, blood and water until smooth; add to boiling broth, stirring constantly. Stir in meat and fruit and heat thoroughly. Serve with boiled potatoes or noodles.

Split Pea Soup

"This is Mother's recipe. She made her pea soup with hamburger instead of the more traditional ham."

Dianne Musil—Columbus

1 package (16 oz.) **Split Peas**, sorted and rinsed
6-8 cups **Water**
1 cup diced **Carrots**
1 **Onion**, chopped
1 cup chopped **Celery**
1 1/2 lbs. **Ground Beef**
Salt and **Pepper** to taste

In a large saucepan, cook peas in water for 30 minutes. Stir in vegetables and beef and continue to cook, stirring occasionally, for 2-2 1/2 hours or until peas are tender. Add more water if needed and season with salt and pepper.

Oven Beef Stew

"This recipe was given to me many years ago by a dear friend."

Betty Henry—St. Paul

2 lbs. **Beef Stew Meat**, cubed
Garlic Powder to taste
3 large stalks of **Celery**, cut into 1-inch pieces
2 **Onions**, quartered
6 **Carrots**, cut into 1-inch pieces
2 large **Potatoes**, cut into 1-inch pieces
2 tbsp. **Minute® Tapioca**
1 tbsp. **Sugar**
3/4 cup **Tomato Sauce**
1/2 cup **Burgandy**
Salt and **Pepper** to taste

Season beef cubes lightly with garlic powder. In a bowl, combine remaining ingredients and mix well. Place vegetable mixture and beef in a roasting pan and mix together. Bake, covered, at 400 degrees for 15 minutes. Reduce temperature to 250 degrees and continue to bake for an additional 4 hours. Do not uncover stew until end of cooking time!

Beef Barley Soup

"This is a combination of ingredients from my other soups."

Lois Mueller—Albion

1 tbsp. **Vegetable Oil**
1 lb. **Beef Stew Meat**, cut into 1-inch cubes
8 cups **Water**
1/2 cup **Hot Water**
2 **Beef Bouillon Cubes**
1 can (16 oz.) **Stewed Tomatoes**
1 cup sliced **Carrots**
1 cup chopped **Onion**
1 cup sliced **Celery**
1/4 cup chopped **Green Bell Pepper**
1 cup chopped **Cabbage**
1 1/2 tsp. **Salt**
1 tsp. **Pepper**

In a large soup pot, heat oil and brown beef. Add water; bring to a boil and simmer over low heat for 1 hour. Remove beef and shred; set aside. In a cup, combine hot water and bouillon and stir to dissolve; add to the soup. Stir in vegetables, salt and pepper. Stir in beef. Cover and continue to simmer for 1 1/2-2 hours or until vegetables are tender.

Potato Cheese Soup

Ruth Brown—Falls City

2 cups **Water**
2 cups diced **Potatoes**
1/2 cup diced **Carrots**
1/2 cup diced **Celery**
1/4 cup chopped **Onion**
1 tsp. **Salt**
1/4 tsp. **Pepper**
1/4 cup **Butter**
1/4 cup **Flour**
2 cups **Milk**
2 cups shredded **Sharp Cheddar Cheese**
1 cup cubed, cooked **Ham**

In a soup pot, bring water to a boil. Add vegetables, salt and pepper. Cook over medium heat for 10 minutes. Meanwhile, in a saucepan, melt butter. Add flour and cook, stirring constantly, until well-blended and mixture begins to turn golden. Gradually stir in milk. Continue to cook, stirring frequently, until thickened. Remove from heat. Add cheddar cheese and stir until cheese is melted; return to heat to melt cheese. Stir in ham and vegetables with broth. Heat thoroughly.

24-Hour Salad

"This recipe is from my sister-in-law who grew up in Geneva. She always brings this to family reunion dinners."

Faye Cool—Merna

Dressing:

3 **Egg Yolks**
2 tbsp. **Sugar**
2 tbsp. **Vinegar**
2 tbsp. **Pineapple Juice**
1 tbsp. **Butter**
Dash of **Salt**
1 cup **Whipped Cream** or
  1 carton (8 oz.) **Cool Whip**®

Salad:

2 cups pitted **White Cherries**
2 cups **Pineapple Chunks** or **Tidbits**, drained
2 **Oranges**, cut into pieces, or 1 can (11 oz.) **Mandarin Oranges**, drained
1 bottle (6 oz.) **Maraschino Cherries**, chopped
2 cups **Miniature Marshmallows**
1 cup diced **Walnuts** (optional)

In a medium saucepan, combine dressing ingredients and cook over low heat for several minutes or until thickened; cool. Place salad ingredients in a salad bowl, fold in dressing and mix well. Cover and refrigerate for 24 hours.

Nebraska State Capitals

Two Nebraska cities claim state capital status: Eustis—sausage and Randolph—honey.

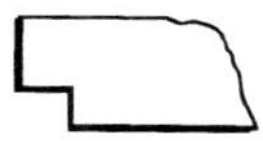

Pasta Salad

"This is a family favorite for all summer gatherings and especially good when made with homegrown vegetables. For variation, try different colors of noodles."

Amber Talbott—Hoskins

1 package (8 oz.) **Spiral Noodles**, cooked and cooled
1 **Green Bell Pepper**, diced
2 **Cucumbers**, diced
1/4 cup diced **Onion**
2 **Tomatoes**, diced

In a salad bowl, combine noodles with vegetables and mix gently. In a saucepan, combine remaining ingredients and bring to a boil; allow to cool. Pour dressing over noodles and vegetables. Toss to coat. Refrigerate at least 4 hours.

Mary's Spinach Salad

"My sister-in-law gave me this recipe many years ago. I especially like it because you can make it a day ahead. Wherever I take this dish, someone always requests the recipe."

Opal Griebel—Cedar Ro Farm, Milburn

Dressing:

1/4 cup **Sour Cream**
3/4 cup **Mayonnaise**
1 tbsp. chopped **Parsley**
1 tbsp. chopped **Chives**

Salad:

6 cups **Fresh Spinach**
1 cup grated **Swiss Cheese**
1/2 cup crumbled, crisp **Bacon**
1 small **Red Onion**, sliced
1/2 cup chopped **Ham**

In a small bowl, combine dressing ingredients and mix well. Set aside. Place half of the spinach in a salad bowl. Layer Swiss cheese, 1/4 cup bacon, onion and ham on top. Cover with remaining spinach and drizzle with dressing. Add remaining bacon and toss gently.

Did You Know?

Buffalo Bill Cody held his first rodeo, the "Old Glory Blowout," in North Platte on July 4, 1882.

Vegetable Salad

Helen Fleischman—Tekamah

- 2 bunches **Broccoli**
- 1 head **Cauliflower**
- 1 **Red Onion**, chopped
- 1 small bunch **Radishes**, sliced
- 2 stalks **Celery**, sliced
- 1 cup **Sour Cream**
- 1 cup **Mayonnaise**
- 2 tbsp. **Red Wine Vinegar**
- 2 tbsp. **Sugar**
- **Salt** to taste

Rinse broccoli and cauliflower and cut into florets; place in a large bowl. Add onion, radishes and celery. In a separate bowl, mix together sour cream, mayonnaise, vinegar, sugar and salt. Pour dressing over vegetables and toss to coat. Refrigerate for at least 1 hour.

Mountain Dew Salad

Teresa Wehling—Custer Public Power District, Broken Bow

- 2 packages (3 oz. ea.) **Lemon** or **Pineapple** Jell-O®
- 2 cups **Boiling Water**
- 1/2 cup **Pineapple Juice**
- 1 cup **Cold Mountain Dew**®
- 1 can (21 oz.) **Lemon Pie Filling**
- 1 cup **Cool Whip**®

In a bowl, dissolve Jell-O in hot water. Add juice and Mountain Dew; stir and let set until slightly thickened. Stir in pie filling. Fold in Cool Whip. Chill.

Egg Nog Salad

"This holiday salad has been a family favorite for two generations."

Doris Gill—Sargent

1 package (3 oz.) **Vanilla Pudding** (do not use instant)
1 box (3 oz.) **Lemon Jell-O**®
3 cups **Hot Water**
2 tbsp. **Lemon Juice**
1 box (3 oz.) **Raspberry Jell-O**®
1 can (16 oz.) **Whole Cranberry Sauce**
1/2 cup diced **Celery**
1/4 cup chopped **Nuts** (optional)
1 carton (8 oz.) **Cool Whip**®
1/4-1/2 tsp. **Nutmeg**

In a saucepan, combine pudding and lemon gelatin with 2 cups of hot water and bring to a boil. Stir in lemon juice. Remove from heat, let cool and pour into a bowl. Refrigerate until partially set. In a separate bowl, dissolve raspberry gelatin in remaining hot water; beat in cranberry sauce. Fold in celery and nuts. Refrigerate until partially set. Add nutmeg to Cool Whip and mix gently. Fold Cool Whip mixture into the pudding. Pour 1/2 of the pudding into an 8 × 8 baking dish. Cover with cranberry mixture; top with remaining pudding. Refrigerate for several hours or overnight.

Main Dishes

Busy Body Roast

"My mother came from Czechoslovakia and may have brought the original version of this recipe with her. As I have served in several capacities in the beef industry, including a term as President of the Nebraska CowBelles (now Cattlewomen), I know that beef doesn't always have to be steak to be delicious as well as nutritious."

Helen B. Clifford—Clifford Partnership, Atkinson

1 (5 lb.) **Beef Pot Roast**
5 cloves **Garlic**, slivered
1 can (10.75 oz.) **Cream of Mushroom Soup**
2 tbsp. **Worcestershire Sauce**
1 package (2.5 oz.) **Lipton® Onion Soup Mix**
Salt and **Pepper** to taste

Place roast beef on a large sheet of aluminum foil. Cut slits in roast and insert slivered garlic. Spread mushroom soup over roast; sprinkle with Worcestershire sauce and onion soup mix; add salt and pepper. Seal foil loosely over roast and place in a roasting pan. Bake at 250 degrees for 10 hours or cook, without foil, in a covered crockpot on low heat for 10 hours.

Steak Diane

Omaha Steaks®—Omaha

2 (6 oz. ea.) **Omaha Steaks® Filet Mignons**
1/8 tsp. **Salt**
1/8 tsp. **Pepper**
2 tbsp. **Butter**
1 tsp. **Dijon-Style Mustard**
2 tbsp. minced **Shallots**
1 tbsp. **Butter**
1 tbsp. **Lemon Juice**
1 1/2 tsp. **Worcestershire Sauce**
1 tbsp. minced **Fresh Chives**
1 tsp. **Brandy**
1 tbsp. minced **Fresh Parsley**

Season both sides of steak with salt and pepper. In a heavy skillet, melt butter; add mustard and shallots and sauté over medium heat for 1 minute. Add steaks and cook 3 minutes per side for medium-rare. Remove steaks to serving plate and keep warm. Add butter, lemon juice, Worcestershire sauce and chives to skillet and cook for 2 minutes. Add brandy and pour sauce over steaks. Sprinkle parsley over tops.

White Turkey Chili

Nebraska Department of Agriculture—Omaha

1 tbsp. **Oil**
1 cup chopped **Onion**
1 cup chopped **Celery**
4 cups chopped, cooked **Turkey**
2 cans (15.5 oz. ea.) **Great Northern Beans**, drained
2 cans (11 oz. ea.) **White Shoepeg Corn**, undrained
1 can (4 oz.) chopped **Green Chiles**
4 cups Turkey or **Chicken Broth**
1 tsp. **Ground Cumin**

Heat oil in a skillet over medium heat. Add onion and celery, and sauté until onion is translucent. Place all ingredients in a large saucepan (at least 4-quart). Stir well. Cover and cook about 15 minutes over medium heat, stirring occasionally, until thoroughly heated.

Alternate cooking method: Place all ingredients in a crock pot and cook on low for approximately 6-8 hours.

Goulash & Dumplings

"My grandmother and mother made this many times. My grandmother came from the Czech Republic in 1907. This dish closely resembles their Czech-style goulash and dumplings."

Helen Macoubrie—Bellwood

1 tbsp. **Shortening**
1 1/2 cups cubed **Stew Beef**
1 small **Onion**, finely chopped
3 cups **Water** or **Beef Broth**
4 tbsp. **Vinegar**
4 tbsp. **Sugar**
1/2 tsp. **Cloves**
1/4 tsp. **Allspice**
Salt and **Pepper** to taste
2 tbsp. **Flour**
1/2 cup **Water**
2 cups **Ketchup**
1 tsp. **Cinnamon**

Dumplings:

2 cups **Flour**
2 tsp. **Baking Powder**
1/2 tsp. **Salt**
2 **Eggs**
1/2 cup **Milk**

In a large skillet, melt shortening; brown beef and onions. Stir in water and simmer for 10 minutes. Pour mixture into a soup pot. Add vinegar, sugar, spices, salt and pepper and cook over medium-low heat for 1/2 hour. In a small bowl, dissolve flour in water and stir into goulash to thicken. Add ketchup and chili powder and mix well. In a bowl, combine dumpling ingredients and mix well. Form dough into 12-15 small balls. In a saucepan, bring water to a boil; drop in dumplings and cook for 10-15 minutes. Serve goulash over dumplings. Serves 4-6.

Omaha—The Crossroads of the Nation

Omaha, the largest city in Nebraska, is one of the world's leading cattle markets and has some of the nation's busiest railroad terminals. Omaha's name is derived from the Omaha Indian language, meaning "above all others on a stream." Father Flanagan's Boys Town and the Henry Doorly Zoo are favorite tourist destinations. Included in the zoo complex are the Lied Jungle, Scott Aquarium and Desert Dome.

Beef & Potato Casserole

"This is really delicious."

Margaret Jasinski—Lincoln

1 lb. **Ground Beef**
Salt and **Pepper** to taste
4 **Potatoes**, peeled and sliced
1 can (10.75 oz.) **Cream of Chicken Soup**
Velveeta®, thickly sliced

In a casserole dish, break up ground beef. Add salt and pepper. Layer potatoes on top of ground beef and spread soup on top of potatoes. Bake, covered, at 400 degrees for 1 hour. Layer top with Velveeta; cover and bake until cheese melts. Serve warm. Serves 4.

Did You Know?

Nebraska's name comes from the Oto Indian word nebrathka, meaning "flat water."

Jessica's Chicken

"A friend gave me this recipe a long time ago. My family has always loved it. It's very easy to make!"

MaryAnne Bazis—Omaha

8 slices **Bacon**, partially cooked
8 skinless, boneless **Chicken Breast Halves**
1 jar (2.5 oz.) **Dried Beef**, chopped
2 cans (10.75 oz. ea.) **Cream of Mushroom Soup**
1 cup **Sour Cream**
1 cup sautéed **Mushrooms**
Parsley Sprigs
3 cups hot, cooked **Rice**

Wrap 1 slice of bacon around each piece of chicken. Place side by side in a greased 12 × 8 baking dish; sprinkle with dried beef. In a bowl, combine soup and sour cream and pour over chicken. Bake at 225 degrees for 3 1/2 hours. Garnish with sautéed mushrooms and parsley sprigs. Serve over rice. Serves 8.

Swedish Potato Bologna Meatballs

"My husband's family, who are of Swedish ancestry, eat potato bologna at special family gatherings. In the early 1900s, potato bologna was homemade in sausage casing. In later years, it was purchased from a grocery store that sells Swedish foods at Christmas time. While doing genealogical research, I found a recipe for potato bologna and adapted it to meatballs. Many family members say it tastes like the homemade potato bologna they remember from their childhood."

Karen Helberg—Callaway

2 **Potatoes**
1 small **Onion**
3/4 tsp. **Allspice**
1/2 tsp. **Salt**
Pepper to taste
Garlic Powder to taste
1 lb. **Ground** Pork
1 lb. **Ground Beef**

Peel and grind potatoes and onion. In a large bowl, combine potatoes, onion, allspice, salt, pepper and garlic powder. Add meat and mix well; refrigerate until firm. Form mixture into small meatballs. Place in a 13 x 9 baking pan; add water to pan to 3/4 inch deep. Bake, covered, at 350 degrees for 1 hour and 5 minutes or until done. Serve with peas and new potatoes. Serves 8.

Grand Island

In 1857, an expedition of 35 German immigrants from Iowa began their settlement in an area along the Platte River the French fur traders called "La Grande Island." Today this city continues to thrive. The Stuhr Museum of the Prairie Pioneer tells the remarkable story of pioneer life. This 200-acre facility includes the boyhood home of Henry Fonda and living-history presentations depicting life on the Great Plains in the 1890s, with costumed interpreters demonstrating such skills as blacksmithing, tinsmithing and dressmaking.

Grilled Beef Steak & Colorful Peppers

National Beef Council/Nebraska Beef Council—Lincoln

2 (2 1/2 lb.) **Beef Porterhouse** or
T-Bone Steaks, cut 1 inch thick
2 small **Red, Yellow** or
Green Bell Peppers, quartered

Parsley Pesto:

1/2 cup packed **Fresh Italian Parsley** Leaves
4 large cloves **Garlic**, minced
3 tbsp. **Olive Oil**

Place pesto ingredients in small bowl of food processor or blender container. Cover; process until finely chopped. Spread pesto on beef steaks and bell peppers. Place steaks and peppers on grid over medium, ash-covered coals. Grill steaks, uncovered, 14- 16 minutes for medium rare to medium doneness and until peppers are tender, turning occasionally. Carve steaks. Season with salt and pepper. Serve with peppers on the side. Serves 4.

Oven-Style Smoked Turkey

Agnes A. Placzek—Columbus

1 (14 lb.) Turkey, thawed

Brine:

2 cups **Tenderquick**®
2 gal. **Water**
1 bottle (3.5 oz.) **Liquid Smoke**
1 cup **Canning Salt**

Remove giblets, neck and tail. In a large container, combine brine ingredients and stir until dissolved. Immerse turkey in brine by placing a plate on top of turkey and adding a weight to the plate to hold turkey down. Refrigerate for 24-36 hours, turning twice. Remove turkey and rinse with water. (Turkey can be refrigerated for 2-3 hours before baking.) Place turkey in a roasting pan and cover. Bake at 300 degrees for 2 1/2-3 hours or until juices run clear. Cool for at least 30 minutes before cutting. Serves 6-8.

Taco Salad

"This dish is served at all of our family reunions!"

Maxine McCarthy—McCarthy Farms, Naper

1 lb. **Ground Beef**, browned
1 can (15.5 oz.) **Kidney Beans**, drained
1 head **Lettuce**, shredded
2-3 **Tomatoes**, chopped
1 **Onion**, chopped
2 cups shredded **Cheddar Cheese**
1 bottle (8 oz.) **Ranch Dressing**
1 bottle (8 oz.) **Green Goddess Dressing**
1 bag (14 oz.) **Doritos® Nacho Cheese Chips**

In a large mixing bowl, combine ground beef, beans, lettuce, tomatoes, onion and cheese. Stir in dressings and mix well; refrigerate. Just before serving, crush chips and gently mix into the salad. Serves 8-10.

Sarma

(Stuffed Cabbage Rolls)

"I received this Croatian recipe from my mother."

MaryAnne Bazis—Omaha

Filling:

2 lb. **Ground Pork Butt**
1/2 lb. **Ground Veal** or **Lean Ground Beef**
1/2 lb. **Bacon**, ground
1 **Onion**, ground
1 clove **Garlic**, minced
1 1/2 cups **Rice**
Salt and **Pepper** to taste

1 head **Cabbage**
1 can (32 oz.) **Sauerkraut**

In a large bowl, combine pork, veal, bacon and onion. Add garlic, rice, salt and pepper and mix well. Wilt cabbage leaves under hot water and place in a pan of simmering water for 30 seconds to soften. Put 2 tablespoons filling on each cabbage leaf and roll up, tucking in ends. Layer cabbage rolls in a large kettle with sauerkraut between layers. Cover with water. Simmer over low heat for 2 hours. Serve with plain boiled potatoes. Serves 6-8.

Creamy Pasta with Ham & Broccoli

"This is a truly wonderful dish. My grandchildren beg for it."

Mary Jo Karnopp—McCool Junction

8 oz. uncooked **Rotini Pasta**
1 tbsp. **Butter**
2 tbsp. **Vegetable Oil**
8 oz. **Fresh Mushrooms**, sliced
2 cloves **Garlic**, minced
2 cups cooked, cubed **Ham**
2 cups **Broccoli**
1 cup **Heavy Cream**
1/4 cup grated **Romano Cheese**

In a large saucepan, cook pasta according to package directions; drain and set aside. Meanwhile, in a large skillet, melt butter; add oil and sauté mushrooms until browned. Add garlic and stir for 30 seconds. Stir in ham, broccoli, cream and Romano cheese and mix. Cook over low heat until sauce thickens slightly. Add pasta, toss lightly and heat through. Serves 4.

Round Steak Supreme

"This is an easy dish to prepare and makes a less tender cut of meat taste great!"

Bonnie G. Clifford—Atkinson

2 tbsp. **Flour**
1 1/2 tsp. **Salt**
1/4 tsp. **Pepper**
2 lbs. **Beef Round Steak,** 1/2-inch thick
3 tbsp. **Oil**
1/2 cup **Water**
1 clove **Garlic**, minced
1 can (15 oz.) **Tomato Sauce**
1 **Green Bell Pepper**, cut into strips
1 **Onion**, sliced
1/2 lb. **Mushrooms**, sliced
2 tsp. **Sugar**
1/2 tsp. **Oregano**
1/4 tsp. **Basil**
1 package (7 oz.) uncooked **Spaghetti**
1/4 cup **Parmesan Cheese**

In a wide shallow dish, combine flour, salt and pepper. Cut round steak into 6 serving-size pieces and dredge in seasoned flour. In a large skillet, heat oil and brown both sides of the steak; drain. Add water and garlic and cook, covered, over low heat for 1 hour. Add tomato sauce, bell pepper, onion, mushrooms, sugar, oregano and basil. Reduce heat and continue cooking for 1/2 hour or until meat is tender. In a saucepan, prepare spaghetti according to directions on package. Serve steak over spaghetti and sprinkle with Parmesan cheese.

Scottsbluff

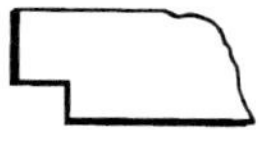

Located in the fertile valley of the North Platte River and on the Western Trails Scenic and Historic Byway, this city is a major trading center for western Nebraska. Just south is the 3,000-acre Scotts Bluff National Monument (yes, the spelling is different!). The bluff was a prominent landmark on the Oregon Trail.

Beef & Kidney Bean Casserole

"I like to serve this dish with hot biscuits."

Lois Mueller—Albion

1 1/2 lbs. **Ground Beef**
1/4 cup chopped **Onion**
1/4 cup chopped **Green Bell Pepper**
1 can (15.5 oz.) **Kidney Beans**, rinsed
1 can (16 oz.) **Stewed Tomatoes**, chopped
3/4 cup cooked **Macaroni**
1 tbsp. **Worcestershire Sauce**
Salt and **Pepper** to taste
Dash of **Sugar**
Dash of **Chili Powder**

In a large skillet, brown the ground beef and sauté onion and bell pepper; drain. Stir in the remaining ingredients and mix well. Pour into a baking dish and bake at 325 degrees for 1 hour. Serves 8.

Grandpa's Beans

"My grandfather passed this recipe down to my father, and he passed it on down to me. We all spent a lot of time outdoors hunting and fishing. This is a good, hearty meal. Now, my daughter makes this dish for family picnics and potlucks."

Terry D. Friesz—Friesz Enterprises, Richland

1/2 lb. **Bacon**, chopped
1/2 lb. **Ground Beef**
1 **Onion**, chopped
1/4 cup packed Brown **Sugar**
1 tbsp. Mustard
2 cans (15 oz. ea.) **Butter Beans**
2 cans (15.5 oz. ea.) **Kidney Beans**
1 can (21 oz.) **Pork & Beans**
1-2 **Potatoes**, boiled and diced (optional)
1/2 bottle (18 oz.) **Barbecue Sauce**

In a large skillet, brown bacon and ground beef. Add onion and sauté until onion is translucent; drain. Add the remaining ingredients and mix well. Pour mixture into a crockpot and cook on low for 4-5 hours. Serves 6.

Mom's Barbecue

"This is a recipe my mother gave to me 24 years ago."

Nancy Burbach—Countryside Home, Newman Grove

1 1/2 lbs. **Ground Beef**
1/2 cup chopped **Onion**
1/4 cup chopped **Green Bell Pepper**
1/8 cup chopped **Celery**
Salt and **Pepper** to taste
1/2 tbsp. **Vinegar**
1 tsp. **Dry Mustard**
3/4 cup **Ketchup**
1/2 cup **Quick Oats**
1 tbsp. **Sugar**
1 tsp. **Chili Powder**
1 can (8 oz.) **Tomato Sauce**
Hamburger Buns

In a large skillet, brown ground beef with onion, bell pepper and celery; drain. Season with salt and pepper. Stir in remaining ingredients and mix well. Bake at 250 degrees for 45-60 minutes, stirring occasionally. Serve on hamburger buns.

Parmesan Herb Pheasant

"With a golden Parmesan cheese and herb coating on tender pheasant, this recipe makes a tempting and hearty main dish. Pheasant and quail are two of Nebraska's hunting favorites."

Bonnie Dytrych—Multi Services Co., Kearney

2 cups grated **Parmesan Cheese**
1/4 cup minced **Fresh Parsley**
2 tbsp. **Oregano**
2 tsp. **Paprika**
1 tsp. **Salt**
1 tsp. **Pepper**
6 **Pheasant Breasts**, bone-in and halved
1 cup **Butter**, melted

In a shallow baking dish, combine the first 6 ingredients and mix well. Dip pheasant in butter and dredge in Parmesan mixture. Place in two greased 15 × 10 baking pans. Bake, uncovered, at 350 degrees for 40-45 minutes or until juices run clear. Serves 12.

Cowboy Casserole

"This was originally cooked over an open fire by Ida Davison Ferrin on her father's ranch on the Wind River Reservation in Wyoming. It was often shared with visiting Sioux, Pawnee, Shoshone and Arapaho."

Frieda Kindler—David City

5 large **Potatoes**, thinly sliced
Salt and **Pepper** to taste
1 **Onion**, diced
1-1 1/2 lbs. **Ground Beef**
1 can (28 oz.) **Pork & Beans**
1/2 cup packed **Brown Sugar**
1/2 cup **Ketchup**

In a buttered 3-quart baking dish, layer potatoes on the bottom and add salt and pepper. Sprinkle half of the onion on top. Break up ground beef on top of onion, then salt and pepper again. Sprinkle the remaining onion over the beef. Pour pork and beans on top. In a small bowl, combine brown sugar and ketchup and spread over casserole. Bake, covered, at 350 degrees for 1 hour. Uncover and bake for an additional 30 minutes.

Sloppy Joes

"Once, when I didn't have a package of the seasoning mix, I came up with this recipe. Our family liked it better, so this is how I make Sloppy Joes now."

Margaret Bradley—Brewster

1 1/2 lbs. **Ground Beef**
1 can (8 oz.) **Tomato Sauce**
3 tbsp. minced **Onion**
5 tsp. **Worcestershire Sauce**
3 tbsp. **Ketchup**
1/4 cup slivered **Green Bell Pepper**
1 tsp. **Celery Salt**
Pepper to taste
Hamburger Buns

In a large skillet, brown ground beef; drain. Stir in the remaining ingredients and mix well. Simmer over low heat for 20-30 minutes. Serve on hamburger buns. Serves 4-6.

Renae's Mexican Casserole

"My husband and I live on a small beef ranch in northeast Nebraska, just south of the South Dakota border. We are the third generation of Vogts to live here. Kelly's grandfather bought the original ranch in 1943. A friend from the local Cattlewomen's Association gave this recipe to me. I have fixed it for my family, visiting hunters and potlucks we attend during the year. It is so easy to make and a delicious way to use Nebraska beef."

Lois A. Vogt—Vogt Ranch, Naper

2 lbs. **Ground Beef**
1/2 cup chopped **Onion**
1 can (10.75 oz.) **Cream of Chicken Soup**
1 can (10.75 oz.) **Cream of Mushroom Soup**
1 can (20-28 oz.) **Mild or Hot Enchilada Sauce**
12 (8-inch) Flour **Tortillas**
2-3 cups shredded **Cheddar** or **Colby-Jack Cheese**

In a large skillet, brown ground beef and sauté onion; drain. In a large bowl, combine beef mixture, chicken soup, mushroom soup and enchilada sauce and mix well. Line a greased 13 x 9 baking pan with 6 tortillas, so that they overlap in the middle and come partially up the sides of the pan. Spread half of the beef mixture over the tortillas. Place remaining tortillas over beef mixture, also making sure they come partially up the sides of the pan. Spread remaining beef mixture over second layer; sprinkle with cheese. Bake at 350 degrees for 25-30 minutes or until cheese is melted. Serves 8-10.

Norfolk

Visit the Elkhorn Valley Museum here to view many exhibits, one of which features native son Johnny Carson of "The Tonight Show." The Hall family of Hallmark Cards and Thurl Ravenscroft, the voice of "Tony the Tiger," are also former residents. Norfolk is home to the state's only steel mill and one of the largest livestock auctions in the world.

Taco Pie Supreme

"This was a favorite when young folks gathered here to visit our daughters during their high school days years ago. This is a quick meal, served with a salad—always a taste-pleaser."

Doris Gill—Sargent

1 lb. **Ground Beef**
1/2 **Onion**, diced
1 can (8 oz.) **Tomato Sauce**
1 pack (1.25 oz.) **Taco Seasoning**
1 tube (15.5 oz.) **Refrigerated Crescent Rolls**
2 cups crushed **Doritos**® **Corn** Chips
1 cup **Sour Cream**
1 cup shredded **Cheddar Cheese**

In a large skillet, break up ground beef and cook with onion until browned; drain. Stir in tomato sauce and taco seasoning. Simmer over medium heat until heated through. Arrange crescent roll dough on the bottom of a greased 9 × 9 baking pan to form crust; sprinkle with 1 cup Doritos. Spoon meat mixture evenly over Doritos; spread sour cream on top. Sprinkle with cheddar cheese and top with remaining Doritos. Bake at 350 degrees for 20-25 minutes.

Beef Steak Casserole

"My mother, Lucy Anderjaska, gave me this recipe. It's very easy to make. We raise cattle on our farm, and besides sending it to market, we share our beef with many members of our family."

Claire Uerling—Indianola

2-3 lbs. **Chuck** or **Sirloin Steak**
1 package (5.4 oz.) **Onion Soup Mix**
1 can (16 oz.) **Diced Tomatoes**
2 tbsp. **Cooking Oil**
2 tbsp. **Wine Vinegar**
Salt and **Pepper** to taste
Garlic Powder to taste

Arrange steak in a large casserole dish. Sprinkle soup mix on top. Add tomatoes; sprinkle with oil and vinegar. Add salt, pepper and garlic powder. Bake at 350 degrees for 1 1/2 hours or until steak is tender.

Wild Rice Casserole

"We serve this at our annual January cookout with family and friends."

Deb Wiegert—Beemer

1 cup uncooked **Wild Rice**
2 cups uncooked **Brown Rice**
2 lbs. **Ground Beef**
1/2 cup **Butter**
1 cup chopped **Onion**
3/4 cup chopped **Celery**
2 cups **Sour Cream**
1/4 cup **Soy Sauce**
2 tsp. **Salt**
1/4 tsp. **Pepper**
2 cans (4 oz. ea.) **Mushrooms**, undrained
1/2 cup **Slivered Almonds**

In large separate saucepans, cook wild rice and brown rice according to directions on the packages. Meanwhile, in a large skillet, brown ground beef; drain and set aside. In the same skillet, melt butter and sauté onion and celery until onion is translucent; add ground beef. In a large bowl, combine sour cream, soy sauce, salt and pepper. Stir in ground beef mixture, wild rice and brown rice and mix well. Add mushrooms and almonds and toss lightly. Pour into a buttered 3-quart casserole*. Bake, uncovered, at 350 degrees for 1 hour. Stir several times during baking, adding more water and seasoning as needed. Serves 6-8.

*If preferred, refrigerate casserole and increase baking time by 15 minutes. Freezes well.

North Platte

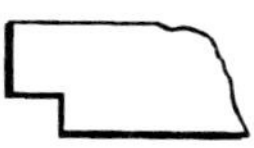

Originally a construction camp for Union Pacific Railroad workers, this town was also home to Colonel William "Buffalo Bill" Cody. Visit his home in the Buffalo Bill State Historical Park and view mementos from his Wild West show. Here, too, is the Lincoln County Historical Museum and Village, featuring original homesteads, a train depot, schoolhouse, church, log cabin, general store, barbership, blacksmith shop and a 200-pound fossil of an 8 to 9-million-year-old land tortoise!

Turkey Meat Loaf

"This is a friend's recipe that I revised to use Egg Beaters® instead of an egg. This makes excellent sandwiches, too!"

Agnes J. Smedra—Kearney

2 lbs. **Ground Turkey** or **Chicken**
1 cup **Quick Oats**
1 medium **Onion**, chopped or 1 tbsp. dried **Onion**
1/2 cup shredded **Carrots**
1/2 cup **Skim Milk**
1/4 cup **Egg Beaters®**
2 tbsp. **Ketchup**
1/2 tsp. **Garlic Powder**
Salt and **Pepper** to taste

Topping:

1/4 cup **Ketchup**
1/4 cup **Quick Oats**

In a large bowl, combine all meatloaf ingredients and mix well. Press mixture into a 9-inch loaf pan. In a small bowl, combine topping ingredients and spread over top. Bake, uncovered, at 350 degrees for 1 hour.

Son-of-a-Gun Beef Stew

"My recipe was printed in a Nebrelles Angus Auxiliary Cookbook in the 1960s. I prepared this recipe in many demonstrations throughout Nebraska. I even made it on television at our state capitol."

Donice Bruner—David City

2 lbs. (1/2-inch thick) **Chuck Steak**
1 tbsp. **Oil**
1 small **Tomato**, sliced
1 medium **Onion**, finely chopped
2 tbsp. **Sour Cream**
1 tbsp. **Flour**
1/2 cup **Hot Water**
1 can (3 oz.) **Mushrooms**
Salt and **Pepper** to taste

Cut steak into small cubes. In a large skillet, heat oil and brown the steak; add tomato and onion. Cook until meat is lightly browned and tender. Stir in sour cream. Sprinkle flour over all and stir to blend well. Add hot water and cook over medium heat, stirring constantly until gravy forms. Stir in mushrooms and add salt and pepper. Serve immediately with fluffy rice or dumplings.

Kraut Runza

(Beef and Cabbage-Filled Rolls)

"This German recipe was passed down from my great-grandmother. This is a tradition of Germans in Nebraska and a 'must' in Nebraska menus."

Sharol Griess—Sutton

Filling:

3 lbs. **Ground Beef**
1 large head **Cabbage**, shredded
1 large **Onion**, thinly sliced
Salt and **Pepper** to taste

Dough:

1 package (.25 oz.) **Yeast**
2 cups **Milk** or **Water**
1/2 cup **Sugar**
1/2 cup **Shortening**
1 tsp. **Salt**
2 **Eggs**, beaten
7-8 cups **Flour**

In a skillet, brown ground beef; add cabbage, onion, salt and pepper. Cook over medium heat until cabbage is tender; set aside to cool. In a large bowl, soften yeast in milk. Add remaining dough ingredients and mix well. Let rise until double in bulk; punch down and let rise again. Turn dough onto a lightly floured surface. Divide in half and roll out to 3/8-inch thickness; cut into 6-inch squares. Place 2 tablespoons filling in the middle of each square, fold dough over and pinch closed. Place squares on a baking sheet and bake at 350 degrees for 20 minutes or until golden brown.

Kearney

The city of Kearney (KAR-nee) was named for Fort Kearney, a government outpost established to protect Oregon Trail pioneers, overland stages, gold prospectors and railroad construction crews. Exhibits at the Great Platte River Road Archway Monument recreate the pioneers' westward journey and pay tribute to America's freedom of mobility. In season, the Kearney area is a stopping point and temporary home for millions of sandhill cranes, whooping cranes, bald eagles, snow geese, ducks, shorebirds and other migratory birds.

Chicken Supreme

"My mother wrote to her sister in Poole, Nebraska, for her 'Chicken Supreme' recipe. I have the letter and recipe my aunt sent in March 1947."

LaVon L. Mason—Custer Public Power, Sargent

1 (3-4 lb.) **Chicken**
Salt and **Pepper** to taste
10 **Eggs**
2 cups **Bread Crumbs**
1/4 cup **Butter**, melted

In a soup pot, cover chicken with water and boil until tender; remove from pot and reserve broth. Let chicken cool, then remove meat from bones and shred. Add to pot. Sprinkle with salt and pepper. In a bowl, beat eggs and stir in 1/2 cup of the hot broth. Pour mixture into soup pot. Bring to a boil and cook for 2-3 minutes until thickened or "clabbered"; remove from heat. Butter a 13 × 9 baking dish and press 1 cup bread crumbs into the bottom and up the sides. Pour chicken mixture into baking dish. In a small bowl, combine remaining bread crumbs with melted butter; sprinkle on top of chicken. Bake at 350 degrees for 10-15 minutes or until center is heated through and bread crumbs are golden brown. Serves 4-6.

The Nebraska State Fair

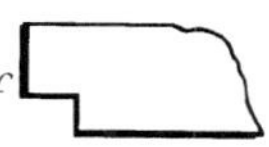

The Nebraska State Fair, held each year in Lincoln during the 10 days prior to Labor Day, offers hundreds of attractions, including entertainers, exhibits, midway rides and delicious food. With a history as old as the state itself, the Nebraska State Fair combines tradition with innovation to produce an educational and exciting event for the entire family.

Paul's Enchiladas

"Our son came up with this recipe. It is a great crowd-pleaser!"

Agnes A. Placzek—Columbus

Filling:

1 1/2 tbsp. **Oil**
1/2 cup chopped **Green Bell Pepper**
1/2 cup chopped **Red Bell Pepper**
1 cup chopped **Onion**
1 cup shredded **Cheddar Cheese**
1 can (14.5 oz.) **Chicken Broth**
2 cans (10.75 oz. ea.) **Cream of Chicken Soup**
1 cup **Sour Cream** (do not use non-fat)
1 can (4 oz.) diced **Green Chiles**
3 **Jalapeños**, chopped
1 cup sliced **Black Olives**
2 tbsp. **Chili Powder**
2 tsp. **Cumin**
1 cup **Cheddar Cheese**
4 cups cooked **Chicken**, cut into small pieces

12 large or 18 small **Flour Tortillas**
2 cups shredded **Cheddar Cheese**
Black Olives

In a skillet, heat oil and sauté bell pepper and onion until onion is translucent. Stir cheddar cheese into skillet mixture and mix well. In a large bowl, combine remaining ingredients. Add skillet mixture and chicken to bowl and combine thoroughly. Cover and refrigerate at least 2 hours. Reserving about 1/2 cup filling for later use, spread 1 heaping tablespoon of chicken mixture down the center of each tortilla; roll tortillas and place in a shallow baking pan. Bake at 325 degrees for 8-10 minutes. Remove pan from oven and spread reserved filling on top; sprinkle with 2 cups cheese and additional olives. Bake, uncovered, for another 20 minutes.

Side Dishes

Summer Zucchini Casserole

"I enjoy making side dishes because they are so versatile. This is one of my favorites to serve with baked chicken or pork chops. Friends really enjoy this when they come over for dinner."

Helen Syfie—Omaha

2 lbs. **Zucchini**, sliced
1/4 cup chopped **Onion**
1 can (10.75 oz.) **Cream of Chicken Soup**
1 cup **Sour Cream**
1 cup grated **Carrots**
1/2 cup **Unsalted Butter**, melted
1 package (6 oz.) **Chicken Flavored Stuffing Mix**

Preheat oven to 350 degrees. In a large saucepan, bring water to a boil and add zucchini and onion. Cook for 5 minutes; drain well. In a bowl, combine soup, sour cream and carrots. Add zucchini mixture and stir well. In a separate bowl, drizzle butter over stuffing and mix well. Spread 1/2 the stuffing in the bottom of a 13 x 9 baking dish. Spoon zucchini mixture over stuffing; top with remaining stuffing. Bake for 25-30 minutes or until golden brown.

Cheesy Potato Pancakes

"My grandmother made potato pancakes with leftover mashed potatoes. She did not use a written recipe."

Terri Schneider—Beemer

2 cups **Cold Mashed Potatoes**
1 **Egg**, lightly beaten
1/8 tsp. **Garlic Powder**
2 tbsp. finely chopped **Chives**
3/4 cup shredded **Cheddar Cheese**
Olive Oil or **Vegetable Oil**

In a large bowl, combine all ingredients, except olive oil, and mix well. In a large skillet, heat 1/8-inch olive oil over medium heat. For each pancake, carefully spoon 1/3 cup of potato mixture into skillet and press lightly to flatten. Cook for about 5 minutes on each side or until golden brown.

Limestone at Weeping Water

Weeping Water, in southeast Nebraska, is the site of one of the nation's largest and most productive limestone mines.

Creole-Style Green Beans

"This recipe has become one of our family's favorites."

Ada Smith—Battle Creek

6 slices **Bacon**
3/4 cup chopped **Onion**
1/2 cup chopped **Green Bell Pepper**
2 tbsp. **Brown Sugar**
1 tbsp. **Worcestershire Sauce**
2 tbsp. **Flour**
1/2 tsp. **Salt**
1/4 tsp. **Pepper**
1/8 tsp. **Dry Mustard**
1 can (15 oz.) **Tomatoes**
1 can (15 oz.) **Green Beans**, drained

In a large skillet, cook bacon; remove and drain on paper towels. Reserve 3 tablespoons bacon drippings in skillet and add onion and bell pepper; sauté until tender. Stir in brown sugar, Worcestershire sauce, flour, salt, pepper and mustard. Add tomatoes and cook until thickened. Stir in green beans; crumble bacon and add to mixture. Heat thoroughly.

Sour Cream Baked Beans

"This is my mother's recipe. She found it in some old books that belonged to her mother. It is different, tasty and healthy, too!"

Agnes J. Smedra—Kearney

2 cups dried **Navy Beans**
1 cup **Sour Cream**
1 cup canned **Tomatoes**, drained
2 tbsp. **Brown Sugar**
3 tbsp. **Molasses**
1 1/2 tsp. **Salt**
Pepper to taste

In a large saucepan, cover beans with water, bring to a boil and cook until tender; drain. Add remaining ingredients and mix well. Pour mixture into a baking dish and bake at 350 degrees for 2 hours.

Easy Glazed Carrots

"My brother made up this recipe, and even people who don't like carrots come back for seconds. It adds a zing to a rather bland vegetable. It is also fast, easy to prepare and tastes great!"

Donna Koerting—Pierce

2 lbs. **Baby Carrots**
1/4 cup **Water**
1 tbsp. **Butter** or **Margarine**
1 tbsp. **Olive Oil**
2 tbsp. **Brown Sugar**
2 tbsp. **Maple Syrup**
1 package (2.5 oz.) **Onion Soup** Mix
Salt and **Pepper** to taste

In a large microwaveable bowl, combine all ingredients and mix. Microwave on high for 2 minutes. Gently mix again to coat carrots with sauce. Microwave for an additional 6-8 minutes or until carrots are tender.

Note: Regular carrots cut into small pieces may also be used.

Did You Know?

Eggplants are actually a fruit—specifically a berry!

Eggplant Stir-Fry

"I invented this recipe when I wanted eggplant that wasn't fried. It is uniquely different from other recipes using eggplant and provides a good way to use up those extra eggplants that late summer brings."

Linda Giese—West Point

1 tbsp. **Olive Oil**
2-3 medium **Eggplants**, cubed (peeled, if desired)
1 1/2 cups chopped **Onion**
1 **Green Bell Pepper**, julienned
2 cloves **Garlic**, minced
1 can (4 oz.) **Mushrooms**, undrained

In a skillet, heat olive oil; add eggplant, onion, bell pepper and garlic. Sauté over medium heat for 5-8 minutes. Add mushrooms and liquid. Simmer over low heat for 15 minutes, stirring frequently.

Maxine's Sweet & Sour Cabbage

"This is a Czech recipe that came from a friend's mother-in-law."

Kathryn B. Ingerle—Elba

- 1 small head **Cabbage**, cut in wedges
- 2 tbsp. **Sugar**
- 2 tbsp. **Flour**, lightly browned
- 1 tbsp. **Shortening**
- 1/4 cup **Vinegar**
- **Salt** and **Pepper** to taste
- 1/2 tsp. **Caraway Seed** (optional)

In a large saucepan, bring a small amount of water to a boil and cook cabbage until tender; drain. In a small bowl, cut together sugar, flour and shortening. Add to cabbage and cook over low heat until thickened. Stir in remaining ingredients.

Fremont

Original settlers here were lured with the promise of free land, free timber for their cabins and a year's supply of firewood. Nearby Fremont Lakes State Recreation Area has more than 20 lakes and a wide variety of watersports, including fishing, boating and waterskiing.

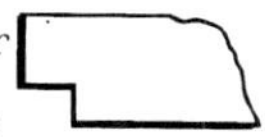

Corn Casserole

"This family favorite came from my daughter-in-law. I make this for our family gatherings–there are never any leftovers."

Alma R. Svoboda—Brainard

- 1 can (15.25 oz.) **Whole Kernel Corn**, undrained
- 1 can (14.75 oz.) **Cream Style Corn**
- 1 1/2 cups shredded **Cheddar Cheese** or **Velveeta®**
- 1 cup broken, uncooked **Spaghetti**
- 1 tbsp. minced **Onion** (optional)
- 1/2 cup **Margarine**, melted

In a 2-quart casserole dish, combine all ingredients and mix well. Bake at 350 degrees for 1 hour.

Holiday Green Beans

"This recipe was passed down from my husband's family. It isn't a holiday now unless Grandma's green beans are made!"

Cindy Brison—Omaha

1/2 cup **Butter**
4 tbsp. **Flour**
1 tsp. **Pepper**
2 cups **Half and Half**
2 lbs. **American Cheese**, cubed
5 cans (14.5 oz. ea.) **Green Beans**
2 tsp. **Tarragon**
1 tsp. **Garlic Powder**
1 tsp. **Seasoned Salt**
1 large **Onion**, peeled and scored
1 can (2.8 oz.) **French-Fried Onion** Rings

In a large saucepan, melt butter and stir in flour. Add pepper. Stir in half and half and cook over medium heat, stirring often, until thickened; add more half and half if too thick. Add cheese and continue to cook until thickened. Drain liquids from 4 of the cans of beans and place all of the beans in a saucepan. Add tarragon and heat; drain. Add beans to cheese mixture, along with the remaining spices. Place the onion in the middle of a large casserole dish and pour the bean mixture on top. Bake at 350 degrees for 30 minutes or until bubbly. Sprinkle onion rings on top 10 minutes before removing from oven.

The Ogallala Aquifer

(oh-ga-la-la)

The Ogallala Aquifer, one of the largest aquifer systems in the world, stretches across about 85% of Nebraska.

Creamy Corn Casserole

"This comforting side dish makes a creamy accompaniment to almost any main course."

Bonnie Dytrych—Multi Services Co., Kearney

2 cans (11 oz. ea.) **Whole Kernel Corn**, drained
1 can (10.75 oz.) **Cream of Celery Soup**
1 cup (8 oz.) **Sour Cream**
1 cup shredded **Cheddar Cheese**
1/2 cup chopped **Celery**
1/2 cup chopped **Onion**
1/4 cup chopped **Green Bell Pepper**
3/4 cup crushed **Butter-Flavored Crackers**
2 tbsp. **Butter**, melted

In a large bowl, combine the first 7 ingredients and mix well. Transfer to a greased 2-quart baking dish; sprinkle with cracker crumbs and drizzle with butter. Bake, uncovered, at 350 degrees for 20-25 minutes or until bubbly.

Pierogi

(Polish Dumplings)

"This is a Polish recipe handed down by my in-laws. I make these at Christmas and Easter to give away as a treat."

Agnes A. Placzek—Columbus

Pierogi:

2 cups **All-Purpose Flour**
1/2 tsp. **Salt**
2 **Eggs**
1/2 cup **Water**

Cottage Cheese Filling:

1 cup **Dry Cottage Cheese**, mashed
1 tsp. **Margarine**
1 **Egg**, beaten
3 tbsp. **Sugar**

2 tbsp. **Butter**

In a bowl, combine flour and salt. In a separate bowl, beat together eggs and water. Combine wet and dry mixtures and mix to form a soft dough. Turn onto a lightly floured surface and knead until smooth; let rest. Combine all filling ingredients and mix well; set aside. Divide dough into egg-size portions. Roll out into 1/8-inch thick circles. Spoon 2 tablespoons of filling into the center of each. Brush one side of dough with water and quickly fold over to form a turnover. Pinch edges of dough to seal tightly; repeat. In a large saucepan, bring salted water to a boil. Carefully add pierogi and cook for 15 minutes; remove and pat dry. In a skillet, melt butter and sauté pierogi until lightly browned.

Note: Pierogi may be frozen, before boiling, on a cookie sheet lined with plastic wrap or waxed paper. Store frozen pierogi in a plastic freezer bag. To use, cook in boiling, salted water for 20-25 minutes; drain. Sauté in butter until lightly browned.

Anna's Turkey Dressing

"In the first years of my marriage, my mother-in-law came over the day before Thanksgiving to help me prepare the turkey stuffing. She didn't have a written recipe, but I created this one from her instructions and still use it today. When I got up early to stuff the turkey, I'd always bake a small dish for the kids' breakfast. This makes enough stuffing for a 20-pound turkey."

Marjorie Klingemann—Ulysses

Turkey Giblets
3/4 cup diced **Onion**
1 1/2 cups diced **Celery**
1/2 tbsp. **Salt**
1 lb. **Butter**
3 cups diced **Apples**
3 cups diced **Potatoes**
3 packages (3 oz. ea.) **Kellogg's® Croutettes® Stuffing Mix**
1 tsp. **Sage**
1 cup **Raisins**
2 1/2 cups **Hot Milk**
Salt and **Pepper** to taste

In a saucepan, combine giblets, onion, celery and salt. Cook until giblets are tender. Remove giblets and set mixture aside. Grind giblets so there are no large chunks. In a large skillet, melt 1 tablespoon butter and cook apples until tender; remove and set aside. In the same skillet, melt another tablespoon butter and cook potatoes until tender. In a large bowl, combine stuffing mix, giblets, apples, potatoes, sage and raisins. In a saucepan, melt remaining butter; stir in giblet broth mixture and then add mixture to stuffing, mixing gently. Stir hot milk into stuffing. Add salt and pepper. Instead of stuffing the turkey, place dressing in a roasting pan and bake in oven at 350 degrees for one hour.

Arbor Day in Nebraska City

Arbor Day, inspired by a resident of Nebraska City, J. Sterling Morton, was first celebrated here in 1872. Statewide, more than 1 million trees were planted on the first Arbor Day. Each year this city celebrates Arbor Day weekend, starting on the last Friday of April, with parades, craft shows and a food festival.

Sauerkraut Casserole

"This is a family favorite. Everyone wants the recipe after they have tasted this casserole. It is truly different and very good!"

Deanna Arbuck—Fairmont

1/2 lb. **Bacon**, cubed
1 **Onion**, chopped
1 can (14 oz.) **Sauerkraut**, drained
1 can (14.5 oz.) **Tomatoes**, drained
1/2 cup packed **Brown Sugar**

In a large skillet, cook bacon until crisp; remove bacon and pour off drippings (except for 2 tablespoons). Add onion to skillet and sauté until translucent. In a bowl, combine onion and bacon, with remaining ingredients and mix well. Place in a casserole dish and bake at 325 degrees for 1 hour and 20 minutes. Serves 4-6.

Columbus

Founded in 1856, this city features the 630-acre Wilkinson Wildlife Management Area, a 31-acre historic district of nearly 100 buildings, and the Andrew Jackson Higgins National Memorial. Higgins designed the special flat-bottomed vessels that helped launch the D-Day attack on Normandy Beach.

Potpourri

(Pickles, Jams, Jellies Frozen Corn & more!)

Garlic Dill Pickles

"This recipe was handed down to me from my mother."

Helen A. Jisa—Dwight

8 sprigs of **Dill**
8 Cloves **Garlic**
Cucumbers (3 to 5-inch) to fill 4 quart jars

Brine:

14 cups **Water**
6 cups **Vinegar**
1/2 cup **Canning Salt**
1 tsp. **Alum**
1/4 cup **Sugar**

Sterilize 4 wide-mouth quart jars. Place 1 sprig of dill and 2 cloves of garlic in the bottom of each jar. Pack with cucumbers. In a large kettle, combine brine ingredients and bring to a boil. Pour hot brine over cucumbers to fill jars; place 1 sprig of dill on top of pickles before sealing. Seal and process in a hot water bath according to manufacturer's directions. Let stand for 2 weeks before serving.

Bonnie's Zesty Cucumbers

"A friend gave me this recipe. I like it because it is different. These cucumbers are my husband's favorite!"

Opal Griebel—Cedar Ro Farm, Milburn

4 **Cucumbers**, sliced
1 1/2 tsp. **Salt**
1/2 **Onion**, sliced
1/2 tbsp. **Mustard Seed**
1/2 tbsp. **Celery Seed**
1/2 cup **Vinegar**
1/4 cup **Sugar**

In a salad bowl, combine cucumbers, salt and onion and let sit for 1 hour; do not drain. Stir in remaining ingredients and mix gently. This will keep in the refrigerator for several days.

Beatrice

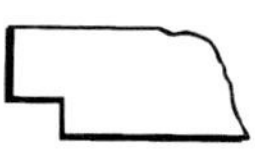

This town's Gage County Courthouse is mentioned in Laura Ingalls Wilder's Little House books. Visit Gage County Historical Museum to view exhibits featuring two native sons: film stars Robert Taylor and Harold Lloyd.

Salt-Free Cucumbers

"I started preparing cucumbers like this when my husband was placed on a salt-free diet."

Marianne Ziethen—Garrison

1/4 cup **Vinegar**
4 tbsp. **Sugar**
Water
Pepper to taste
2-3 **Cucumbers**, sliced
3-5 slices **Onion**

In a measuring cup, combine vinegar and sugar. Add enough water to equal 1 cup. Add pepper. Place cucumbers and onion in a salad bowl and cover with vinegar mixture. Cover and marinate in refrigerator for several hours or overnight.

Old-Fashioned Dill Pickles

"Mom always made these. So did our grandmother. We couldn't wait until they were ready to eat."

Carolyn Wilkens—Gibbon

8 **Grape Leaves** or pinch of **Alum**
8 sprigs of **Dill**
Cucumbers to fill a 2-gallon jar
2/3 cup **Pickling Salt**
10 cups **Water**

Place 4 grape leaves and 4 sprigs dill in a 2-gallon stone jar. Pack cucumbers into the jar until almost full; place remaining grape leaves and dill on top. In a pitcher, combine pickling salt with water and stir to dissolve; pour over cucumbers. Invert a plate and place on top of the jar. Fill a 1-pint jar with water and set it on top of the plate to keep cucumbers immersed in juice. Cover loosely with a clean cloth and let stand for 4 days at room temperature before serving.

Refrigerator Pickles

"This is a recipe my aunt gave me when we lived on the farm. I have shared it with many friends."

LaRue Rehrs—Hampton

- 9 cups unpeeled **Cucumber**, cut in 1/4 inch slices
- 1 cup sliced **Onions**
- 2 tbsp. **Canning Salt**
- 1 tbsp. **Celery Seed**
- 2 cups **Sugar**
- 1 cup **Vinegar**

Place cucumbers and onions in a 1-gallon jar. In a bowl, combine remaining ingredients; stir until blended. Pour mixture over cucumbers, cover and refrigerate. Turn and shake jar several times a day. Pickles will be ready to eat in 5-7 days.

Dad's Favorite Pickled Beets & Eggs

"My mom always made lots of pickled beets. She made a gallon of pickled eggs at a time so we could have this treat for Easter!"

Karen Cline—Culbertson

5 lbs. **Fresh Beets**, tops and roots attached
1 quart **Water**
1 1/2 quarts **Vinegar**
4 cups **Sugar**
2 tbsp. **Canning Salt**
4 sticks **Cinnamon**, broken into small pieces
2 tsp. **Whole Cloves** or 1 tbsp. **Pickling Spice** plus 1 stick **Cinnamon**, tied in a mesh bag
2 dozen **Eggs**

Wash beets thoroughly, leaving the roots and 2 inches of green tops. Place in a large kettle, cover with water and bring to a boil. Cook only until skins peel off easily. Drain (reserving liquids), cool and peel beets, removing tops and roots. Cut into quarters. Add beets to hot, sterilized quart jars until half full. In a saucepan, combine vinegar with sugar and spices and bring to a boil. Pour vinegar mixture over beets to fill jars 1/2 inch from top. Clean rims and seal. Process in water bath for 15 minutes according to manufacturer's directions. In a saucepan, cover eggs with water and cook until hard-boiled; let cool. Peel eggs and place in a jar. Heat reserved beet liquid; pour over eggs and cover and refrigerate for at least 3 days.

Note: Add red food coloring if desired. The eggs and beet liquids may be stored in the refrigerator for up to 1 month.

Hebron

Hebron is the home of the "World's Largest Porch Swing." In this photo, twenty-one Nebraskans enjoy their swing!

Picadilly

(Tomato Relish)

"Mother said that Grandma Gladys Nichelson made the best relish in Saunders County; this is her recipe."

Cindy Prochaska—Dwight

2 gallons finely chopped **Green Tomatoes**
8 large **Onions**, finely chopped
1 head **Cabbage**, finely chopped
3 **Green** or **Red Bell Peppers**, finely chopped
1 cup non-iodized **Salt**

Brine:

2 quarts **Vinegar**
1 tbsp. **Mustard**
2 tbsp. **Cinnamon**
1 tbsp. **Allspice**
2 cups **White Sugar** or packed **Brown Sugar**
2 tbsp. **Ginger**

In a large bowl, combine tomatoes, onions, cabbage and bell peppers; add salt. Let stand overnight; drain well. Press mixture through cheesecloth to remove as much liquid as possible. In a large kettle, combine brine ingredients; add vegetables and bring to a boil. Pour mixture into hot, sterilized jars and seal according to manufacturer's directions.

Yummy Pickled Eggs

"This recipe was created by my good friends, Rick and Chuck."

Nancy Burbach—Countryside Home, Newman Grove

12 **Hard-Boiled Eggs**, peeled
2 cups **White Vinegar**
2 tbsp. **Sugar**
1 cup **Water**
1 tsp. **Salt**
1 tsp. **Garlic Salt**
1-2 cloves **Garlic**, minced

Place eggs in a 2-quart glass jar. In a saucepan, combine vinegar, sugar, water, salt and garlic salt. Bring to a boil. Pour hot mixture over eggs. Add garlic cloves to jar. Cover and refrigerate for 2-3 days before serving.

Grandma's Cinnamon Pickle Rings

"This recipe is from my Grandma Schmit."

Shirley Beetem—St. Paul

1 gal. peeled **Cucumbers**, cut in 1/4 inch slices
1 cup Lime **Juice**
4 1/2 cups **Water**
1/2 cup **Vinegar**
1 oz. **Red** Food Coloring
1/2 tsp. **Alum**

Brine:

1 cup **Vinegar**
5 cups **Sugar**
1 cup **Water**
4 **Cinnamon Sticks**
1/2 large pack **Red Hots® Cinnamon Candies**

Remove centers from cucumber slices. In a bowl, combine lime juice with water and add cucumber. Cover and refrigerate for 24 hours; drain. In a large stainless steel saucepan, combine cucumbers with vinegar, food coloring and alum. Add water to cover. Bring to a simmer and cook over low heat for 2 hours; drain. In a separate saucepan, combine brine ingredients and bring to a boil. Pour over cucumbers; marinate overnight. For 3 days, drain and reheat brine, then pour it back over the cucumbers. Remove cinnamon sticks. Pack pickles into eight hot, sterilized pint jars; add juice to cover and seal according to manufacturer's directions.

Homestead National Monument of America

Located just 40 miles south of Lincoln, this monument commemorates the Homestead Act of 1862, a law that granted 160-acre parcels of free land to men and women moving west. Situated on 100 acres of restored tallgrass prairie, the Monument is a tribute to the strength and courage of Nebraska's homesteaders. Visit an original 1867 cabin and other period buildings and exhibits.

Wild Plum Jelly

Two winning recipes from Dorothy Hillebran of Omaha!

Nebraska State Fair—Lincoln

5 lbs unpeeled, pitted **Wild Plums**, chopped
1 1/2 cups **Water**
1 box (1.75 oz.) **Sure-Jell®**
6 1/2 cups **Sugar**

In a saucepan, cover plums with water and bring to a boil. Reduce heat, cover and simmer 10 minutes, stirring often. Pour mixture into a 3 layer cheesecloth bag, tie closed and let drip into a bowl. Press gently to get out all of the juice. Place 5 1/2 cups plum juice in a 6-quart saucepan; add Sure-Jell. Bring mixture to a boil over high heat; add sugar and stir until dissolved. Return to a rolling boil and boil hard for 1 minute, stirring constantly. Remove pan from heat and skim surface if needed. Ladle hot juice into hot, sterilized jars, leaving 1/2-inch head space. Adjust two piece caps. Process for 5 minutes in a boiling water canner.

Hastings

The Hastings Museum is home to the J. M. McDonald Planetarium and the Lied Super Screen Theatre. Another great attraction is the historic Jacob Fisher Rainbow Fountain whose many changing colors of lights accompany the varying arrays of water sprays that reach heights of 67 feet!

Wild Plum Butter

4 quarts unpeeled, pitted **Wild Plums**
2 3/4 cups **Sugar**

In a saucepan, cover plums with water and boil until skins are tender. Put mixture through a sieve and then return pulp and juice to saucepan. Stirring constantly, add sugar and boil mixture until it reaches a jelly-like consistency. Seal in hot, sterilized jars and process 10 minutes in a boiling water canner.

Tomato Preserves

"Since I work in our well-drilling business, I love to freeze and can foods to use when I am in a hurry."

Claudeen Penry—Elkhorn Valley Drilling, Inc., Atkinson

3 large **Yellow** or **Red Tomatoes**, peeled and diced
3 cups **Sugar**
1 tbsp. **Real Lemon® Lemon Juice**
1 box (3 oz.) **Lemon** or **Orange Jell-O®**

In a large saucepan, combine tomatoes, sugar and juice and bring to a boil. Reduce heat and cook slowly over low heat until tomatoes are tender. Add Jell-O and stir to dissolve. Pour mixture into hot, sterilized jars and seal according to manufacturer's directions.

Note: Whole cloves or cinnamon sticks can be added while cooking.

Frozen Sweet Corn

"My dad was a dry land farmer. Every year, when he planted his field corn, he would also plant a section of sweet corn. We picked the corn, husked and froze it so we could have corn all year long."

Liana Rich—Culbertson

2 quarts **Corn**, cut from cobs
1 quart **Water**
1/4 cup **Sugar**
4 tsp. **Salt**

In a large saucepan, combine all the ingredients and bring to a boil. Reduce heat and simmer over low heat for 10 minutes, stirring often; let cool. Divide into desired portions, spoon into freezer bags or containers, label and freeze.

Corn Cob Jelly

"I collect red field corn cobs during harvesting for this jelly."

Karen Christensen—Berwyn

14 large **Corn Cobs**
1 package (3 oz.) **Sure-Jell®**
3 cups **Sugar**

In a saucepan, cover corn cobs with water and boil for 30 minutes. Strain 3 cups of the corn liquid into a separate saucepan. Add Sure-Jell and stir to dissolve. Bring mixture to a hard boil and boil for 1 minute. Stir in sugar and boil for an additional minute; set aside. Skim off foam. Pour mixture into two sterilized pint jars and refrigerate.

Crab Apple Jelly

"During the Depression, my mother-in-law used the fruit from a flowering crab apple tree to make this jelly. It made pretty Christmas gifts for teachers and friends."

Marjorie Klingemann—Ulysses

Crab Apples, washed and halved
Sugar

In a saucepan, cover apples with water and cook until tender; strain and reserve juice. Measure juice and add an equal amount of sugar. In a separate saucepan, cook juice mixture over medium heat for about 20 minutes, until it jells; pour over apples. Pour mixture into hot, sterilized jelly glasses and seal according to manufacturer's directions.

Movies Made in Nebraska

A few of the movies made in Nebraska include: Boys Town, Men of Boys Town, Sea of Grass, Airport, Paper Moon, The Chisolms, The Long Run, Terms of Endearment, Miracle of the Heart, Home at Last, Trial of Standing Bear and About Schmidt.

Rhubarb-Pineapple Jam

"So much rhubarb is grown in Nebraska, this must have been an original Nebraskan recipe."

Norma Doescher—West Point

5 cups chopped **Rhubarb**
4 cups **Sugar**
1 can (8.5 oz.) **Crushed Pineapple, with Juice**
1 package (3 oz.) **Orange Jell-O®**

In a large kettle, combine rhubarb and sugar, stir and let stand overnight. Add pineapple and juice and bring to a boil. Cook over high heat for 10 minutes, stirring often. Remove from heat, add Jell-O and stir until dissolved. Pour into hot, sterilized jars and seal according to the manufacturer's directions.

"Blubarb" Jam

"This is my mother's recipe. It is one of those 'pass-around' recipes. Friends and neighbors keep asking for it."

Faye Cool—Merna

5 cups **Rhubarb**, cut in 1-inch pieces
5 cups **Sugar**
1 can (21 oz.) **Blueberry Pie Filling**
1 package (6 oz.) **Raspberry-Flavor Gelatin**

In a large saucepan, cook rhubarb in a small amount of water just until tender. Add sugar and pie filling and stir until sugar is dissolved. Cook over low heat for 10 minutes, stirring often to prevent scorching. Stir in gelatin. Pour into hot, sterilized jars and seal according to manufacturer's directions. Makes 4 pints.

Farm Fresh Rhubarb Jam

"This recipe is from my mother-in law. She made rhubarb jam every spring. It is very good on ice cream as well as toast."

Trudy Rief—West Point

9 cups diced **Rhubarb**
7 cups **Sugar**
1 bx. (3 oz.) **Raspberry or Strawberry Jell-O®**

In a large saucepan, combine rhubarb and sugar; cook, stirring often, over low heat until rhubarb is tender and juicy. Bring to a boil and cook for 2 minutes. Add Jell-O and stir until dissolved. Pour into hot, sterilized jars and seal according to manufacturer's directions. Makes 8 pints.

Breads

Kolaches

(Sweet Filled Yeast Rolls)

"My mother is of Czech descent. Her recipe calls for a fruit filling, but Kolaches can be made with a variety of fillings."

Lois J. Higgins—Newport

Kolache Dough:

2 packages (.25 oz. ea.) **Yeast**
1 pint **Milk**, scalded
3/4 cup **Sugar**
3 **Eggs**, beaten
1/2 cup **Lukewarm Water**
3/4 cup **Shortening**
2 tsp. **Salt**
8 cups **Flour**
Cherries, Plums, Apricots or **Peaches**, for filling

Topping:

1/2 cup **Sugar**
1/2 cup **Flour**
1-2 tbsp. **Lard**

In a large bowl, combine yeast, milk and sugar; set aside until yeast is foamy. Add eggs, water and shortening. Gradually add salt and flour and mix well to form a slightly sticky dough. Let rise until double in size; punch down and allow to rise again. Form into 2-inch balls. Flatten balls on a greased cookie sheet and let rise again. Prepare your choice of fruit filling according to your favorite recipe. Make an indentation in the center of each kolache and add a tablespoon of filling. Cut topping ingredients together until crumbly and sprinkle evenly over filling. Bake at 350 degrees for 20-25 minutes.

Bohemian Christmas Bread

"My parents brought this recipe with them from Bohemia."

Olga Strong—Strong Insurance, Gordon

1/2 lb. **Dried Prunes**
1/2 lb. **Dried Pears**
7 cups **Flour**
1/2 cup **Butter**
2 packages (.25 oz. ea.) **Yeast**
1 tsp. **Salt**
1/2 cup **Sugar**
1 **Egg**, beaten
1/2 tbsp. **Cinnamon**
1/2 tbsp. **Cloves**
1 cup coarsely chopped **Nuts**
1/2 cup **Raisins**
1/2 cup **Golden Raisins**
1/2 cup **Currants**
1/2 cup chopped **Figs**
1 cup chopped **Dates**
Glazed Fruits to taste
1 box **Hot Roll Mix**

In a saucepan, cover prunes and pears with water and cook until soft; drain (reserving juice) and chop. In a bowl, mix flour, butter, yeast, salt, sugar, egg and 3 1/2 cups reserved juice. Leave for about 15 minutes in a warm place. Add remaining ingredients, except hot roll mix, and mix well. Let rise until double in size. Knead lightly. Form into 2-4 loaves, depending on the pan sizes. Prepare roll mix according to directions on box. Roll a portion of this dough into a thin sheet with a rolling pin. Wrap the hot roll dough around each loaf of fruit bread. Bake at 300 degrees for 1-1 1/2 hours, depending on the size of the loaves, or until toothpick inserted in center comes out clean. Turn off oven, leaving loaves inside for a few minutes, and then remove to wire racks. Allow bread to cool completely before slicing.

Note: Prune and pear juice will make a dark dough. If lighter dough is preferred, use 3 cups of milk and 1/2 cup of water.

Lake Minatare

One of the most popular and scenic recreation areas in Nebraska's Panhandle, Lake Minatare State Recreation Area encompasses 2,973 acres, including the 2,158-acre reservoir. The 55-foot-tall lighthouse at Lake Minatare is one of only seven inland lighthouses in the country.

Cream Cheese Banana Bread

"This has been a neighborhood favorite for many years."

Sylvia Soule—Harrisburg

- 4 **Eggs**
- 1 cup **Margarine**
- 2 cups **Sugar**
- 1 package (8 oz.) **Cream Cheese**, softened
- 1 tsp. **Vanilla**
- 2 tsp. **Lemon Juice**
- 1 tsp. **Maple Extract**
- 1/4 tsp. **Cinnamon**
- 1/2 cup **Wheat Germ**
- 3 1/2 cups **Flour**
- 2 tsp. **Baking Powder**
- 2 tsp. **Baking Soda**
- 5-6 ripe **Bananas**, mashed
- 1 cup chopped **Nuts**

In a large bowl, cream together eggs, margarine, sugar and cream cheese. Add vanilla, lemon juice, maple extract, cinnamon and wheat germ and mix thoroughly. In a separate bowl, sift together flour, baking powder and baking soda. Add half the flour mixture to the batter. Fold in bananas. Add remaining flour mixture and nuts; mix thoroughly. Pour batter into 2 greased 8 × 4 loaf pans. Bake at 350 degrees for 1-1 1/2 hours or until toothpick inserted in center comes out clean

Rhubarb Bread

Betty Henry—St. Paul

- 2 cups **Sugar**
- 1 cup **Vegetable Oil**
- 3 **Eggs**, lightly beaten
- 2 cups chopped **Rhubarb**
- 1 tbsp. **Vanilla**
- 3 cups All-Purpose **Flour**
- 2 tsp. **Cinnamon**
- 1 tsp. **Baking Powder**
- 1 tsp. **Baking Soda**
- 1 tsp. **Salt**
- 1 cup chopped **Walnuts**

In a mixing bowl, combine sugar, oil and eggs; mix well. Stir in rhubarb and vanilla. In a separate bowl, sift together flour, cinnamon, baking powder, baking soda and salt. Stir into wet mixture until just moistened. Stir in nuts. Pour into 2 greased 8 × 4 loaf pans. Bake at 325 degrees for 55-65 minutes or until toothpick inserted in center comes out clean. Cool 10 minutes in pans and then remove to a wire rack.

Swedish Rye Bread

"Stromsburg is a Swedish community and my family is Swedish. We love this rye bread recipe."

Ramona Teegerstrom—Stromsburg

1 package (.25 oz.) **Yeast**
2 1/4 cups **Lukewarm Water**
1 **Egg**, beaten
1/2 cup **Molasses**
2 tbsp. **Shortening**
1/2 cup **Sugar**
1 tsp. **Salt**
1 tbsp. **Caraway Seed**
6 cups **All-Purpose Flour**
2 1/2 cups Rye **Flour**

In a small bowl, dissolve yeast in 1/4 cup warm water. In a separate mixing bowl, combine remaining warm water, egg, molasses, shortening, sugar, salt and caraway seeds. Add yeast mixture and mix using an electric mixer. Stir in both types of flour and knead again until smooth and elastic. Let rise until double in size; punch down and divide into two loaves. Place loaves in greased 9 × 5 loaf pans; let rise again until double in size. Bake at 400 degrees for 10 minutes; reduce heat to 350 degrees and bake for 40-45 minutes. Remove from pans and brush with butter.

Heavenly Cloud Biscuits

"These biscuits are very light and flaky. The secret to their melt-in-the-mouth goodness is an egg and a smidgen of sugar."

Betty Dowse—David City

2 cups **Flour**
1 tbsp. **Sugar**
4 tsp. **Baking Powder**
1/2 tsp. **Salt**
1/2 cup **Margarine**
1 **Egg**, beaten
2/3 cup **Milk**

In a large mixing bowl, sift together dry ingredients; cut in shortening until mixture is crumbly. In a separate bowl, combine egg and milk; add to flour mixture all at once. Stir until dough is sticky. Turn out onto a lightly floured surface; knead gently with heel of hand for about 20 strokes. Roll dough out to 3/4-inch thickness. Cut with a round cookie cutter and place on an ungreased baking sheet 3/4 inch apart. If desired, chill 1-3 hours. Bake at 450 degrees for 10-14 minutes or until golden brown.

Norwegian Apple Muffins

Anne Anderson—Gothenburg

4 tbsp. **Margarine**
1 cup **Sugar**
1 **Egg**
2 1/4 cups **Flour**
3 1/2 tsp. **Baking Powder**
1/2 tsp. **Salt**
1/4 tsp. **Cinnamon**
1/4 tsp. **Nutmeg**
1 cup **Milk**
1 cup finely chopped **Apples**

Topping:

2 tbsp. **Sugar**
1/4 tsp. **Cinnamon**
1/4 tsp. **Nutmeg**

In a bowl, cream together margarine and sugar; add egg and beat well. In a separate bowl, sift together flour, baking powder, salt, cinnamon and nutmeg. Add dry ingredients to creamed mixture; blend in milk and then fold in apples. In a small bowl, combine all topping ingredients. Fill muffin cups about 3/4 full and sprinkle with topping. Bake at 375 degrees for 20 minutes.

The Cowboy Trail: *The Nation's Longest Rail-to-Trail Project*

Created in the 1870s as a route to Black Hills gold, this 321-mile railroad corridor between Chadron and Norfolk has become the nation's longest recreational rail-to-trail project. The eight-foot wide trail includes more than 200 bridges. One, over a quarter-mile long and 148 feet high, spans the Niobrara River, one of the nation's top ten canoeing rivers. Today, only a little over 100 miles of the trail are open, but construction continues daily. For maps and information, contact the Nebraska Game and Parks Office (402) 471-5511 or visit their website: www.outdoornebraska.org.

Zweiback

"This bread was brought from Germany by my ancestors who came to the U.S. in 1876. Many homes in our Mennonite community still make these rolls every Saturday."

Arlyce M. Friesen—Henderson

4 tbsp. **Dry Yeast**
4 cups **Warm Water**
1/4 cup **Sugar**
1 cup Dry **Milk**
1/2 cup **Shortening**
1/2 cup **Butter**
2 tbsp. **Salt**
10-12 cups **Flour**

In a large mixing bowl, mix yeast, warm water and sugar; stir until yeast has dissolved. Add dry milk, shortening, butter and salt; mix thoroughly. Slowly add the flour until spoon can no longer be used, then work in enough flour with hands until dough is just past the cohesive stage. Knead briskly for 2-3 minutes. Place in a greased bowl, cover and set in a warm area. Allow dough to rise until doubled in size. Punch down and allow to rise again. Shape half of the dough into 2-inch rounds and the balance into 1 3/4-inch rounds. Place the larger rounds on a lightly greased baking pan. Press the smaller rounds firmly down onto the top of the larger rounds. Let rise for 15 minutes. Bake at 425 degrees for 10-12 minutes or until golden.

Cream Drop Biscuits

"This is my grandmother's recipe taken from her own handwriting. She always cooked these biscuits in a wood stove."

Eileen Brown—Atkinson

2 cups **Flour**
3 tsp. **Baking Powder**
1 tsp. **Sugar**
1/2 tsp. **Salt**
2/3 cup **Heavy Cream**
1/3 cup **Milk**

In a bowl, sift together dry ingredients. In a separate bowl, combine heavy cream and milk. Stir dry ingredients into cream mixture until soft dough forms. Drop onto a greased baking sheet and bake at 450 degrees for 12-14 minutes or until golden brown.

Stollen

(German Christmas Bread)

"This recipe was handed down to my mother from my grandmother who emigrated from Germany. I like to make these smaller leaves for Christmas gifts."

LaRue Rehrs—Hampton

2 packages (.25 oz. ea.) **Yeast**
1/2 cup **Warm Water**
2 1/2 cups **Milk**
2 cups **Sugar**
2 tsp. **Salt**
1 cup **Butter**
Juice and grated **Peel of** 1 **Lemon**
4 **Eggs**, beaten
1 lb. **Golden Raisins**
2 lbs. **Raisins**
1/4 lb. **Prunes**, cooked and chopped
1 cup chopped **Almonds**
8-10 cups **Flour**

In a small bowl, dissolve yeast in warm water. In a saucepan, scald milk. Add sugar, salt and butter; remove from heat and cool to lukewarm. Transfer to a large bowl and add lemon juice and peel, eggs, raisins, prunes and almonds. Add flour to make a stiff dough. Knead until smooth. Place dough in a greased bowl, cover and keep warm. Allow to rise overnight. In the morning, punch down and form into 6-8 loaves. Place loaves in 5 × 3 loaf pans and let rise again until doubled. Bake at 250 degrees for 1 hour or less, until golden. Remove from oven and place on cooling rack. Brush with melted butter and sprinkle with sugar.

Bran Bread

"I remember Mother making this bread when I was a child."

Suzanne Bryant—Tekamah

2 cups **Kellogg's® All-Bran**
1 cup **Flour**
2/3 cup **Sugar**
Pinch of **Salt**
1 1/2 cups **ButterMilk** or **Sour Milk**
1 tsp. **Baking Soda**
1/2 cup **Raisins**

In a bowl, combine all ingredients in order given. Pour into 1 (9 × 5) or 2 (7 × 3) loaf pans. Bake at 350 degrees for 40-45 minutes, until tests done.

Grandma's Küchen

(German Coffee Cake)

"My maternal grandmother, Freda Nicolaus, was of German descent. She would make this coffee cake and freeze it so she would have plenty on hand for unexpected guests."

Lois A. Vogt—Vogt Ranch, Naper

Cake:

1 package (.25 oz.) **Yeast**
1/2 cup **Warm Water**
1 tsp. **Sugar**
1 **Egg**, beaten
1/2 cup **Milk**
1/4 cup **Margarine**
1/3 cup **Sugar**
1/2 tsp. **Salt**
4 cups **Flour**

Filling:

1 can (12 oz.) **Evaporated Milk**
3-4 **Eggs**
2 tbsp. **Sugar** (or to taste)
Sliced **Apples**, Peaches, **Apricots** or **Prunes**

In a small bowl, dissolve yeast in water. Stir in 1 teaspoon sugar and egg; set aside. In a saucepan, bring milk and margarine to a boil, stirring frequently. Remove from heat and, when cool, pour into a large bowl; stir in 1/3 cup sugar and salt. Add yeast mixture and gradually mix in flour to create a soft dough; let rise until double in bulk. In a bowl, beat together filling ingredients. Divide dough into four sections; roll each section into thin 9-inch rounds. Lightly press into greased 9-inch pie pans. Add filling and layer fruit on top. Place pie pans on cookie sheets and bake at 350 degrees for 30 minutes or until center tests done.

Bertha's Pumpkin Cornbread

"This is different and delicious!"

Opal Griebel—Cedar Ro Farm, Milburn

1 1/2 cups **Whole-Wheat Flour**
1 cup **Yellow Cornmeal**
2 tsp. **Baking Powder**
1 tsp. **Baking Soda**
1 tsp. **Cinnamon**
1/2 tsp. **Nutmeg**
1/4 tsp. **Cloves**
1/4 tsp. **Salt**
1/2 cup **Butter**, softened
2/3 cup packed **Brown Sugar**
4 **Eggs**
1 cup **Canned Pumpkin**
1 cup **Milk**

In a bowl, combine dry ingredients. In a separate mixing bowl, beat butter for 30 seconds. Add brown sugar and cream until fluffy. Add eggs and pumpkin and beat on low speed until well-blended. Add dry ingredients and milk alternately to creamed mixture. Continue beating until combined. Pour into a greased 9 × 5 loaf pan. Bake at 350 degrees for 1 hour. Cool in pan for 10 minutes. Remove from pan and cool completely.

Ashfall Fossil Beds State Historical Park

This fossil site in northern Antelope County contains hundreds of skeletons of prehistoric animals in a volcanic ash bed. Some of the best-preserved fossil rhinos, three-toed horses, camels, sabre-toothed deer and birds have been, and are being, excavated by museum crews. It is truly a "time capsule," presenting us with a picture of a vanished world more than 10 million years old!

Farm-Style Biscuits

"My mother's family homesteaded in Custer County. Biscuits were a staple in Nebraska farm life. You had them for breakfast with syrup or honey, for dinner as your main bread and for supper with beef or sausage gravy."

Kaye Einspahr—Enders

2 cups **Flour**
4 tsp. **Baking Powder**
2 tsp. **Sugar**
1/4 tsp. **Salt**
1/2 tsp. **Cream of Tartar**
1/2 cup **Margarine**
2/3 cup **Milk**
1 **Egg**

In a mixing bowl, combine all dry ingredients. Cut margarine into dry ingredients until crumbly. Add milk and egg all at once. Stir until dough leaves the side of the bowl. Turn dough onto a lightly floured surface and pat to a 3/4-inch thickness. Cut out rounds with a biscuit cutter. Place on a greased baking sheet and bake at 450 degrees for 10-12 minutes until golden brown.

Ice Box Biscuits

"I have used this recipe for many years."

Eileen Brown—Atkinson

1 package (.25 oz.) **Yeast**
1/2 cup **Sugar**
1 cup **Warm Water**
1/2 tsp. **Salt**
3 **Eggs**
3/4 cup **Margarine**, melted
4 cups **Flour**

In a large bowl, dissolve yeast in water. Let stand until foamy. Stir in sugar, salt, eggs and margarine. Add flour and mix well. Cover and refrigerate overnight. On a heavily floured surface, roll out dough to 1/4-inch thickness. Cut out a 12-inch circle then cut into wedges like pieces of a pie. Roll from the wide end to the point of each wedge and place on a greased cookie sheet. Let stand, covered, until raised. Bake at 375 degrees for about 15 minutes, until golden.

New Penny Puff Rolls

"I try other roll recipes occasionally, but this one is the best!"

Kathryn B. Ingerle—Elba

1 tbsp. **Yeast**
1 tsp. **Sugar**
1/2 cup **Lukewarm Water**
1/2 cup **Margarine**
1/2 cup **Shortening**
1 cup **Boiled Potato Water**
1 cup **Water**
1/2 cup **Dry Milk**
1 tbsp. **Salt**
1/2 cup **Sugar**
7 cups **Flour**
3 **Egg Yolks**
1 tbsp. **Vanilla**

In a small bowl, dissolve yeast and sugar in water; set aside. In a saucepan, melt margarine and shortening. Stir in potato water, plain water, dry milk, salt and sugar; heat until milk is dissolved. Sift 3 cups flour into a large mixing bowl; add potato water mixture and beat well. Add yeast mixture, egg yolks and vanilla and beat again. Slowly add remaining flour. Put in a greased bowl and grease top of dough. Let rise until double in size; punch down and let rise again. Roll into balls and place on a greased cookie sheet. Let rise for 15 minutes. Bake at 400 degrees for 12-15 minutes, until golden brown. Brush with melted butter.

Desserts

Bohemian Apple Strudel

"This is my Czechoslovakian grandmother's recipe."

Bonnie Kadavy—Weston

1/3 cup **Cold Water**
1 1/2 tbsp. **Shortening**
1 **Egg**, slightly beaten
1 1/2 cups **Flour**
Pinch of **Salt**
1 tsp. **Sugar**
1/4 cup **Margarine**, cut into small pieces

In a bowl, beat together water, shortening and egg. Add flour, salt and sugar and mix until well-blended. Knead on a lightly floured surface until dough is smooth and elastic. Return to bowl and allow to stand in a warm place for 45 minutes. Place dough on a large cloth dusted with flour and begin stretching dough gradually. Continue until dough is stretched very thin, being careful not to tear the dough. Spread **Apple Filling** over dough and dot with margarine. Roll up carefully jelly roll-style. Seal edges and brush lightly with butter. Bake at 350 degrees for 1 hour or until lightly browned, brushing top with butter every 15 minutes.

Apple Filling:

3/4 cup **Sugar**
1 cup **Bread Crumbs**
1 tsp. **Cinnamon**
1 cup **Raisins**
8 **Apples**, peeled and thinly sliced

In a bowl, combine first four ingredients and mix well. Stir in apples until evenly coated

Mincemeat Pie

"This is my grandmother's recipe.
It's a Thanksgiving and Christmas tradition."

Jo Matulka—Dwight

1 (2 lb.) **Roast**, boiled and ground or
  2 lbs. **Ground Beef**
2 cups **Beef Broth**
9 cups (6-7 lbs.) **Ground Apples**
1 cup chopped **Sour Cherries**
1 lb. packed **Brown Sugar**
1 cup **Sugar**
1 lb. **Raisins**
1/2 lb. **Currants**
1 tsp. **Nutmeg**
1 tsp. **Cloves**
1 tsp. **Allspice**
3 tsp. **Cinnamon**
4 cups **Apple Juice** or **Cherry Juice**
1 tsp. **Salt**
2 unbaked **Pie Crusts**

In a large saucepan, combine all ingredients except pie crusts. Simmer for 2 hours or until apples are tender and mixture thickens. Spread 3-4 cups mincemeat in pie shell (freeze remaining mincemeat for later use). Add top crust; seal edges and vent. Bake at 400 degrees for 45 minutes or until browned.

Chimney Rock

This slender spire soaring some 500 feet up from the Platte River Valley floor signaled to westward bound travelers the end of the prairie and beginning of the rugged high plains. Visit Chimney Rock Visitor Center to learn more about the great westward migrations.

Rhubarb Cake

"When we first see rhubarb in the garden, we are reminded that spring has arrived."

Betty Hoobler—Custer Public Power District, Broken Bow

1 1/2 cups **Sugar**
1/2 cup **Shortening**
1 **Egg**
1 cup **Sour Cream** or **ButterMilk**
2 cups **Flour**
1 tsp. **Baking Soda**
1/4 tsp. **Salt**
1 tsp. **Vanilla**
1 1/2 cups diced **Rhubarb**

Topping:

1/4 cup **Sugar**
2 tsp. **Cinnamon**

In a bowl, cream together sugar and shortening. Add egg and beat well. Mix in sour cream, flour, baking soda, salt and vanilla. Stir in rhubarb and then pour into a greased 13 × 9 pan. Combine topping ingredients and sprinkle over batter. Bake at 350 degrees for 35 minutes or until toothpick inserted in center comes out clean.

Fresh Raspberry Pie

"We grow and sell asparagus and raspberries at our farm. Our customers pick their own raspberries for this delicious pie."

Stephana Spangler—Sunwest Farm, Lincoln

1 cup + 2 tbsp. **Sugar**
2 tbsp. **Cornstarch**
1 cup **Water**
2 tbsp. **Raspberry-Flavored Gelatin**
1 package (8 oz.) **Cream Cheese**
1 tbsp. **Milk**
1 quart **Fresh Raspberries**
1 baked **Pie Shell**

In a saucepan, combine 1 cup sugar, cornstarch and water. Bring to a boil and cook over medium heat until thick and clear. Add gelatin and mix well; cool slightly. In a bowl, beat together cream cheese, remaining sugar and milk. Spread cream cheese mixture in bottom of pie shell. Sprinkle fresh berries over the top and pour gelatin mixture over all. Refrigerate until set.

Did You Know?

Only 6 of Nebraska's 93 counties contain more people than cattle!

Wild Plum Pie

"When the Sandhills were first settled, food was scarce and wild plum thickets grew along many creek banks. The plums were used for sauces and preserves and for pies like this!"

June Wescott—Brewster

2 cups **Sugar**
2 cups **Water**
Pinch of **Cinnamon**
2 tbsp. **Flour**
1 cup pitted, cooked and puréed **Wild Plums**
2 unbaked **Pie Crusts**
2 tbsp. **Butter**

In a saucepan, combine all ingredients and bring to a boil. Simmer over medium heat until thickened. Pour mixture into pie crust and dot with butter. Top with second crust; seal edges and vent. Bake at 375 degrees for 45 minutes or until golden brown.

Grandma Loseke's Cream Pie

"This family favorite comes from my husband's grandmother."

Elaine Chamberlain—Tekamah

2 cups **Sweet Cream**
1 cup **Sugar**
1/8 tsp. **Salt**
1 tsp. **Vanilla**
4 **Egg Whites**
2 unbaked **Pie Shells**

In a bowl, pour cream over sugar. Add salt and vanilla and mix well. In a separate bowl, beat egg whites until stiff peaks form. Fold egg whites into cream mixture. Pour mixture into pie shells and bake at 350 degrees for about 40 minutes, until crusts are light brown and centers are set.

Kudlinky

(Czech Christmas Cookies)

"My grandparents brought this recipe from Czechoslovakia."

Helen A. Jisa—Dwight

6 **Eggs**
2 cups **Sugar**
1/4 tsp. **Salt**
4 + cups **Flour**
Anise **Seed**
Candy Decorations

In a bowl, mix together 5 eggs, sugar and salt. Add enough flour to make a stiff dough. Roll dough out to 1/8 inch thickness and cut with a crimped cookie cutter. In a small bowl, beat remaining egg with 1 tablespoon water. Brush cookies with egg wash and sprinkle with anise seed and candy decorations. Place on a non-stick cookie sheet and bake at 325 degrees for 8-10 minutes or until edges turn light brown. Immediately remove cookies from pan and place across a broom handle that has been covered with a towel. Slightly bend cookies over the handle so cookies are curved. Age for a few days to enhance anise flavor.

Wilber

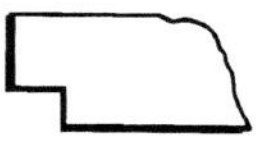

Home of the Miss Czech-Slovak USA Pageant! This city claims the title "Czech Capital of the U.S.A.," and celebrates its annual Czech Festival the 1st full weekend in August.

Mulberry Pie

"My mom used to make this pie. My sisters and I would pick the mulberries off our tree."

Dianne Musil—Columbus

3 cups **Fresh Mulberries**
2 unbaked **Pie Crusts**
2 tbsp. **Cornstarch**
Dash of Salt
1 cup **Sugar**
1 tbsp. **Butter**

Place berries in pie shell. In a small bowl, combine cornstarch, salt and sugar. Sprinkle over berries. Dot with butter and add second crust; seal edges and vent. Bake at 400 degrees for 40-50 minutes, until crust is golden.

Rhubarb-Mulberry Pie

"When I was a child, Mom would make us this treat with fresh rhubarb and mulberries and serve it with homemade ice cream."

Jo Matulka—Dwight

3 cups chopped **Rhubarb**
2 cups **Mulberries**
1 unbaked **Pie Shell**
2 **Eggs**, separated
1 cup **Sugar**
1 cup **Half and Half** or **Evaporated Milk**
1 tbsp. (heaping) **Flour**

Meringue:

4 tbsp. **Sugar**
1/4 tsp. **Cream of** Tartar
2 **Egg** Whites

Spread rhubarb and mulberries in pie shell. In a bowl, beat together egg yolks, sugar, half and half and flour. Pour over fruit. Bake at 350 degrees for 45 minutes or until set; cool. To make meringue: In a small bowl, mix together sugar and cream of tartar. While beating egg whites, add sugar mixture one tablespoon at a time. Beat until stiff peaks form. Spread meringue over pie and return to the oven for 8-10 minutes or until tips of meringue are golden brown.

Rhubarb Custard

"Our rhubarb plants were transported from our grandparents' house to ours after we were married and I had started a garden. This is my husband's favorite rhubarb dessert."

Jan Pogreba—Seward

2 tbsp. + 1 tsp. **Butter**
3 cups chopped **Rhubarb**
1 1/4 cups **Sugar**
2 tbsp. **Cornstarch**
2 **Eggs**
1/4 cup **Milk**
1/8 tsp. **Salt**

In a saucepan, combine 2 tablespoons butter, rhubarb and 1 cup sugar. Cook until rhubarb is tender. In a bowl, whisk together remaining sugar, cornstarch, eggs, milk, salt and remaining butter. Gradually stir custard into rhubarb mixture. Cook, stirring constantly, until thickened. Refrigerate until set.

Potato Candy

"My mother made this recipe for the family when I was growing up. Now I make it for my family. It's one of our favorites."

Ellen Doughty—Columbus

1 **Baking Potato**
Powdered Sugar
Vanilla to taste
1 package (12 oz.) **Semi-Sweet Chocolate Chips**
Shavings of **Parawax**

In a saucepan, cover potato with water and bring to a boil. Simmer until tender; peel and mash while still warm. Add 1/4 cup powdered sugar and a few drops of vanilla and mix well. Let stand until cooled. Add more powdered sugar until mixture is stiff enough to roll into balls the size of walnuts. Let stand again in a cool place (do not refrigerate) until firm. In a saucepan, melt chocolate chips and add a few shavings of parawax. Dip potato balls in chocolate and place on wax paper to cool.

Note: Peppermint or wintergreen extract may be substituted for the vanilla. Ground fruit or nuts may also be added.

Cottage Cheese Pie

"We always made our own cottage cheese when Mother made this pie."

Kathryn B. Ingerle—Elba

1 cup **Cottage Cheese**, drained
1/2 cup **Raisins**
1 unbaked **Pie Shell**
3 **Eggs**, lightly beaten
1/2 cup **Sugar**
1 tsp. **Vanilla**
1/2 tsp. **Salt**
2 cups **Milk**

In a bowl, mix together cottage cheese and raisins; spread in pie shell. In a separate bowl, beat together eggs, sugar, vanilla and salt. In a saucepan, scald milk. Pour milk slowly into egg mixture, stirring constantly. Pour custard over cottage cheese mixture and bake at 350 degrees for 30 minutes or until a toothpick inserted in center comes out clean.

Rhubarb Coffee Cake

"This is a family favorite, handed down for generations. Rhubarb is readily available in every yard in our community and used in a wide variety of recipes."

Doreen M. Novacek—Dwight

2 cups **Flour**
1 1/4 cups **Sugar**
1 tsp. **Baking Soda**
1/2 tsp. **Cinnamon**
1 tsp. **Salt**
1/2 cup **Margarine**
2 cups chopped **Rhubarb**
2 **Eggs**, beaten
1/3 cup **Milk**
1/2 cup chopped **Nuts**
1/2 cup packed **Brown Sugar**

In a bowl, sift together flour, sugar, baking soda, cinnamon and salt. Cut margarine into dry ingredients until crumbly. Reserve 1/2 cup of crumb mixture for topping. Add remaining ingredients, except brown sugar, to crumb mixture and mix well. Pour into a greased and floured 13 × 9 baking pan. Combine reserved crumb mixture and brown sugar. Sprinkle over batter and bake at 350 degrees for 35-40 minutes. Serve warm with ice cream or whipped cream.

About Rhubarb

Though eaten as a fruit, rhubarb is actually a vegetable. The leaves of this red-stalked plant contain oxalic acid and can be toxic. Therefore, all recipes calling for rhubarb are utilizing only the reddish, celery-like stalks.

Poppy Seed Torte

"My mom always found one or two occasions during the year to make this impressive torte."

Tim Vala—Vala's Pumpkin Patch, Gretna

- 3/4 cup **Poppy Seeds**
- 1 cup **Milk**
- 2/3 cup **Butter**
- 1 1/2 cups **Sugar**
- 1 tsp. **Vanilla**
- 2 cups **Flour**
- Dash of **Salt**
- 2 tsp. **Baking Powder**
- 4 **Egg Whites**, beaten stiff

In a small bowl, combine poppy seeds and milk; soak for 2 hours. In a separate bowl, cream together butter and sugar; add vanilla and beat well. In another bowl, combine dry ingredients. Add milk mixture and dry ingredients alternately to creamed mixture, mixing well after each addition. Fold in egg whites. Line bottoms of three (9-inch) cake pans with wax paper. Pour batter into pans and bake at 375 degrees for 20-25 minutes or until centers test done. Remove cakes from oven and cool. Cut each cake in half horizontally. Spread **Walnut Filling** between halves and then stack all three cakes. Frost top and sides with **Chocolate Frosting**.

Walnut Filling:

- 1/2 cup **Sugar**
- 1 1/2 cups **Milk**
- 1 tbsp. **Cornstarch**
- 4 **Egg Yolks**
- 3/4 cup **Walnuts**

In a saucepan, cook sugar, milk and cornstarch over medium heat, stirring often, for 10 minutes. Add a small amount of cooked mixture to egg yolks, then add yolks to saucepan. Cook, stirring constantly, for 1 more minute; cool and add nuts.

Chocolate Frosting:

- 1 1/2 cups **Sugar**
- 6 tbsp. **Milk**
- 6 tbsp. **Margarine**
- 1 tbsp. **Kahlúa**®
- 1/2 cup **Semi-Sweet Chocolate Chips**

In a saucepan, combine sugar, milk and margarine. Bring to a boil for 30 seconds. Add Kahlua and chocolate chips and beat until thick. Cool.

Country-Style Ice Cream

"This is my mom's recipe for the best homemade ice cream!"

Liana Rich—Culbertson

- 5 cups **Milk**
- 2 tbsp. **Flour**
- 1/4 tsp. **Salt**
- 2 1/2 cups **Sugar**
- 4 **Eggs**, beaten
- 4 cups **Whipping Cream**
- 2 tbsp. **Vanilla**

In a heavy saucepan, scald 4 cups milk. In a small bowl, combine remaining milk, flour, salt and sugar; pour into scalded milk. Cook over low heat, stirring constantly, until mixture starts to thicken. Add some of the cooked mixture to eggs, then add egg mixture to cooked mixture; stir over medium-low heat until smooth. Stir in vanilla and cream. Pour into ice cream freezer; freeze according to manufacturer's directions.

Nebraska World Capitals

Three Nebraska cities claim world capital status: Alliance—cattle, Cozad—alfalfa and North Loup—popcorn.

Pfefferneuse

(Christmas Peppernuts)

"My grandmother, Irene Meyer, always made these cookies for Christmas, and all eight of her grandchildren loved them."

Susan Fuoss—Norfolk

2 cups **Sugar**
1 cup **Molasses**
1 1/2 cups **Margarine**
2 **Eggs**
1 tsp. **Cinnamon**
1 tsp. **Nutmeg**
1 tsp. **Cloves**
1 tsp. **Ginger**
1 tsp. **Black Pepper**
1 tsp. **Anise**
1 tsp. **Baking Soda**
1 cup **Hot Water**
4 + cups **Flour**

In a bowl, cream and mix together all ingredients, except baking soda, water and flour. In a small bowl, combine baking soda and hot water and stir; add to sugar mixture. Mix in flour until stiff dough forms. Refrigerate overnight. Roll into 1-inch balls and bake on a greased cookie sheet at 375 degrees for 8-10 minutes.

Red Hot Cherry Pie

"I won a purple ribbon for this in the Dawes County Fair 4-H Pie Contest. It's a dessert that my family continues to enjoy."

Angie E. Hawthorne—Hawthorne Farms, Chadron

2 unbaked (9-inch) **Pie Crusts**
1 can (20 oz.) **Cherry Pie Filling**
1/2 cup **Red Hots**® or other **Cinnamon Candies**
1/3 cup **Coconut Flakes**

Place one pie crust in pie pan. Spread filling in crust and layer red hots and coconut on top. Add second pie crust; crimp edges to seal and vent. Sprinkle top with sugar. Bake at 400 degrees for 15 minutes; decrease heat to 350 degrees and bake another 30 minutes.

Deadhorse Creek Market Pie

with "Gifts of the Orchard" Filling

"I developed this recipe for our farmers market from a recipe of my mother's. It is a community favorite!"

Ava L. Hawthorne—Deadhorse Creek Market-Hawthorne Farms, Chadron

Gifts of the Orchard Filling:

1 can (29 oz.) **Peaches**
1 can (29 oz.) **Pears**
1 can (29 oz.) **Apricots**
3 **Apples**, thinly sliced
1 tbsp. **Butter**
3 tbsp. **Tapioca**
3 tbsp. **Cornstarch**
3/4 cup **Sugar**
Juice of 1 **Orange**
1/4 tsp. **Nutmeg**
Sprinkle of **Cloves**
1/2 tsp. **Cinnamon**

4 (9-inch) unbaked **Pie Crusts**
Dashes of **Cinnamon**

Crumble Topping:

2 sticks **Butter**, softened
2 cups **Sugar**
2 cups **Flour**

Drain canned fruits and cut into small pieces; reserve juices. Combine fruits (including apples) in an 8-cup microwaveable bowl and add butter, tapioca and cornstarch. Stir in sugar and blend all together. Microwave on high for 6 minutes. Stir well; microwave for another 6 minutes. Add remaining ingredients, blend well and microwave another 6 minutes; add reserved juice if needed. Pour fruit mixture into pie shells and cover to the edges with crumble topping. Sprinkle tops with cinnamon and bake at 400 degrees for 15 minutes. Reduce heat to 350 degrees and bake until filling begins to bubble and topping is browned.

Chadron

Chadron is headquarters for many vacation activities and attractions. Chadron State Park is the state's oldest state park, consisting of 950 acres of buttes and wooded hills. Be sure and visit the Museum of the Fur Trade, a famous attraction built on the site of an old trading post.

Zucchini Carrot Cake

"Zucchini cakes and breads have been summer desserts in our family for years since zucchini grows so well in Nebraska. The carrots bring a 'confetti' color and sweetness to this cake."

Harlan R. Musil—Lincoln

3 **Eggs**, beaten
1 cup **Oil**
1 cup packed **Brown Sugar**
1 cup **Sugar**
2 tsp. **Vanilla**
2 cups unpeeled, shredded **Zucchini**
1 cup shredded **Carrots**
3 cups **Flour**
1 tsp. **Baking Soda**
1/2 tsp. **Baking Powder**
1 tsp. **Salt**
1 tsp. **Cinnamon**

In a bowl, combine eggs and oil; add both sugars and vanilla and beat until well-combined. Add zucchini and carrots and mix well. In a separate bowl, sift together dry ingredients; add to wet mixture. Pour batter into a greased and floured 13 × 9 baking pan. Bake at 325 degrees for 1 hour or until tests done. Cool and frost with **Cream Cheese Frosting.**

Cream Cheese Frosting:

1 package (8 oz.) **Cream Cheese**
1/2 cup **Butter** or **Margarine**
1 lb. **Powdered Sugar**
2 tsp. **Vanilla**

In a bowl, beat together all ingredients until smooth.

Paczki

(Filled and Deep-Fried Pastries)

"I remember helping my bushia (grandmother in Polish) make these cookies. Nowadays I make dozens of them for my family."

Marcene Kaslon—Ashton

1 1/4 cups **Sugar**
2 cups **Warm Water**
4 tbsp. **Yeast**
10 **Egg Yolks**
2 tbsp. **Salt**
2 cups **Mashed Potatoes**
1 tbsp. **Almond Extract**
1 1/4 cups **Shortening**
10-12 cups **Flour**
Fruit or **Poppy Seeds**, for filling
Sugar

In a large mixing bowl, combine 1/4 cup sugar, warm water and yeast. Using electric mixer, mix for 30 seconds; let stand until foamy. With mixer on low speed, add egg yolks one at a time. Add remaining sugar, salt, potatoes, almond extract and shortening, mixing well after each addition. Slowly add flour, one cup at a time, until mixture is too thick to use mixer. Add remaining flour, kneading with hands until dough is no longer sticky. Cover bowl and let dough rise until double in size. Place a portion of dough on a lightly floured surface and pat out to a 1/4-inch thickness. With a large glass or a cookie cutter, cut out circles. Place a teaspoon of filling in the center of each circle. Fold in half and seal edges. Repeat process until all dough is used. Let rise for 10 minutes. Fry in a deep-fat fryer, turning once, until rich brown in color. Drain on paper towels and then roll in sugar.

Prairie Schooners and Pioneer Trails

Prairie schooners, half-size versions of Conestoga wagons, were used by early pioneers to cross the United States in the 19th century. They followed many different trails along the Platte and North Platte Rivers as they crossed Nebraska on their way to California's gold fields or to the free land being offered to all pioneers in Oregon.

Cesky Plum Dumplings

"My mother is Bohemian and grew up in eastern Nebraska. When she was young, her mother made these plum dumplings as a special treat."

Mary J. Metzger—Lincoln

3 cups **Mashed Potatoes**
1 tsp. **Salt**
1/4 cup **Farina** or **Cream of Wheat**®
2 **Egg Yolks**
2 cups **Flour**
12-14 Italian or **Blue Plums,** pitted
Melted **Butter**
Toasted Bread Crumbs
Cinnamon-Sugar

In a bowl, mix together potatoes, salt, farina and egg yolks. Add flour and mix well to make a slightly stiff dough. Roll out dough until 1/2-inch thick. Cut into 2-inch squares. Place a plum in the center of each square. Pinch together the corners and roll into balls. Bring a large pot of salted water to a rapid boil. Working in batches, drop dumplings in boiling water and cook for 10-12 minutes. The dumplings will sink to the bottom and then come to the top. Remove from water and roll in melted butter, toasted bread crumbs and then cinnamon-sugar.

Maple Nutties

"This is my mother's recipe for a very unique Christmas cookie. Our walnuts were homegrown."

Lois J. Higgins—Newport

2/3 cup **Butter**
1/4 tsp. **Baking Powder**
1/3 cup **Powdered Sugar**
1 tsp. **Water**
1 tsp. **Maple Extract**
2 cups **Flour**
1 cup finely chopped **Walnuts**
Powdered Sugar

In a bowl, cream butter; slowly adding baking powder and powdered sugar. Add water, maple extract, flour and walnuts. Divide dough into four or more portions and roll into pencil-thin ropes. Cut into pieces 2-3 inches long. Place on a greased cookie sheet and bake at 350 degrees for 15-20 minutes or until golden. Remove from oven and roll in powdered sugar.

Crumble Top Strawberry-Rhubarb Pie

"This recipe is from my mother. I especially like to make it in the spring when the rhubarb is new and strawberries are in season."

Dorothy Heimann—West Point

1 tbsp. **Quick-Cooking Tapioca**
3/4 cup **Sugar**
1 1/2 cups halved **Strawberries**
1 cup uncooked **Oats**
1/2 cup packed **Brown Sugar**
1/2 cup **Flour**
1 tsp. grated **Orange Peel**
1/4 tsp. **Salt**
1/2 cup **Butter**, melted
2 cups chopped **Rhubarb**
1 unbaked **Pie Shell**

In a bowl, combine tapioca, sugar and strawberries; set aside for 15 minutes. In a separate bowl, combine oats, brown sugar, flour, orange peel and salt. Add butter and mix well. Place rhubarb in pie shell. Pour strawberries on top and sprinkle with oat mixture. Bake at 425 degrees for 35-40 minutes.

Brown Pudding

"This is an old family recipe from my mother."

Vickie Welling—Crawford

Dumplings:

1 tbsp. **Margarine**
1/2 cup **Sugar**
1 tsp. **Cinnamon**
1 tsp. **Nutmeg**
Pinch of **Salt**
1/2 cup **Milk**
1 cup **Flour**
2 tsp. **Baking Powder**
1/2 cup **Raisins**

Syrup:

1 1/2 cups packed **Brown Sugar**
1/4 cup **Margarine**
2 1/4 cups **Hot Water**

Cream together the first five ingredients. Add remaining dumpling ingredients and mix to a stiff dough. In a deep 2-quart rangetop casserole dish, bring brown sugar, margarine and hot water to a rapid boil. Carefully drop dough by spoonfuls into boiling syrup. Bake at 350 degrees for 12-15 minutes or until a tooth-pick inserted in center of dumpling comes out clean.

Salsa Lovers Cookbook

More than 180 recipes for salsa, dips, salads, appetizers and more!
$10.95

Quick-n-Easy Mexican Recipes

Make your favorite Mexican dishes in record time! Excellent tacos, tostadas, enchiladas and more!
$10.95

Cowboy Cookbook

Cowboy and western favorites! A great combination of historic and new recipes. Includes cowboy trivia
$10.95

Tortilla Lovers' Cookbook

Celebrate the tortilla with more than 100 easy recipes for breakfast, lunch, dinner, appetizers and desserts, too!
$10.95

Chili Lovers Cookbook

Prize-winning recipes for chili, with or without beans. Plus a variety of taste-tempting foods made with flavorful chile peppers.
$10.95

Pecan Lovers Cookbook

Indulge your pecan passion with pralines, macaroons, ice cream, bread, pudding, muffins, cakes, cookies, main dishes, and a wide variety of pecan pies.
$10.95

Kokopelli's Cookbook

A collection of authentic Southwestern and Native American recipes. More than 50 hand-illustrated reproductions of mimbres pottery, mythology and historical lore.
$10.95

Easy RV Recipes

Easy recipes for the traveling cook. Over 200 recipes to make in your RV, camper or houseboat.
$10.95

Easy Recipes for Wild Game

More than 200 "wild" recipes for large and small game, wild fowl and fish.
$10.95

Apple Lovers Cookbook

What's more American than eating apple pie? Try these 150 favorite recipes for appetizers, main and side dishes, muffins, pies, salads, beverages and preserves.
$10.95

Pumpkin Lovers Cookbook

More than 175 recipes for soups, breads, muffins, pies, cakes, cheesecakes, cookies and even ice cream! Carving tips, trivia and more.
$10.95

Mexican Family Favorites Recipes

250 authentic, homestyle recipes for tacos, tamales, menudo, enchiladas, burros, salsas, frijoles, carne seca, chile rellenos, guacamole, and more!
$10.95

ORDER BLANK

GOLDEN WEST COOKBOOKS

5738 North Central Avenue • Phoenix, AZ 85012

www.GoldenWestCookbooks.com • 1-800-521-9221 • FAX 602-234-3062

Qty	Title	Price	Amount
	Apple Lovers Cookbook	10.95	
	Bean Lovers Cookbook	10.95	
	Berry Lovers Cookbook	10.95	
	Burrito Lovers Cookbook	10.95	
	Chili Lovers' Cookbook	10.95	
	Chip and Dip Lovers Cookbook	10.95	
	Cowboy Cookbook	10.95	
	Date Lovers Cookbook	10.95	
	Easy Recipes for Wild Game & Fish	10.95	
	Easy RV Recipes	10.95	
	Kokopelli Cookbook	10.95	
	Low Fat Mexican Recipes	10.95	
	Mexican Family Favorites Cookbook	10.95	
	Peach Lovers Cookbook	10.95	
	Pecan Lovers Cookbook	10.95	
	Pumpkin Lovers Cookbook	10.95	
	Quick-n-Easy Mexican Recipes	10.95	
	Salsa Lovers Cookbook	10.95	
	Seafood Lovers Cookbook	10.95	
	Squash Lovers Cookbook	10.95	
	Tequila Cookbook	10.95	
	Tortilla Lovers Cookbook	10.95	
	Veggie Lovers Cookbook	10.95	
	Vegi-Mex Vegitarian Recipes	10.95	
	Western Breakfast	10.95	
U.S. Shipping & Handling Add: (Shipping to all other countries see website.)			$ 3.99
	Arizona residents add 8.6% sales tax		

Total $ ______
(Payable in U.S. funds)

☐ My Check or Money Order Enclosed

☐ MasterCard ☐ VISA ☐ Discover ☐ American Express Verification code______

Acct. No.______________________ Exp. Date__________

Signature______________________

Name______________________ Phone__________

Address______________________

City/State/Zip______________________

Call for a FREE catalog of all our titles — Prices subject to change —